FORTRESS • 87

SARACEN STRONGHOLDS 1100–1500

The Central and Eastern Islamic Lands

DAVID NICOLLE

ILLUSTRATED BY ADAM HOOK

Series editors Marcus Cowper and Nikolai Bogdanovic

First published in 2009 by Osprey Publishing
Midland House, West Way, Botley, Oxford OX2 0PH, UK
443 Park Avenue South, New York, NY 10016, USA
E-mail: info@ospreypublishing.com

ISBN: 978 1 84603 375 9
E-book ISBN: 978 1 84908 099 6

Editorial by Ilios Publishing Ltd, Oxford, UK (www.iliospublishing.com)
Cartography: Map Studio, Romsey, UK
Page layout by Ken Vail Graphic Design, Cambridge, UK (kvgd.com)
Typeset in Sabon and Myriad Pro
Index by Auriol Griffith-Jones
Maps by Map Studio Ltd, Romsey, UK
Originated by PPS Grasmere Ltd, Leeds, UK
Printed in China through Bookbuilders

09 10 11 12 13   10 9 8 7 6 5 4 3 2 1

A CIP catalogue record for this book is available from the British Library.

For a catalogue of all books published by Osprey Military and
Aviation please contact:

NORTH AMERICA
Osprey Direct, c/o Random House Distribution Center,
400 Hahn Road, Westminster, MD 21157
Email: uscustomerservice@ospreypublishing.com

ALL OTHER REGIONS
Osprey Direct, The Book Service Ltd, Distribution Centre,
Colchester Road, Frating Green, Colchester, Essex, CO7 7DW, UK
E-mail: customerservice@ospreypublishing.com

www.ospreypublishing.com

DEDICATION

For 'little Katy', greatly missed.

ARTIST'S NOTE

Readers may care to note that the original paintings from which the
colour plates in this book were prepared are available for private sale.
All reproduction copyright whatsoever is retained by the Publishers.
All enquiries should be addressed to:

Scorpio Gallery, PO Box 475, Hailsham, East Sussex BN27 2SL, UK

The Publishers regret that they can enter into no correspondence
upon this matter.

GLOSSARY

ahdath	urban militia (Arabic).
ark	citadel (Farsi).
ashlar	masonry cut to regularly sized and close-fitting blocks.
bab	gate (Arabic).
barid	government postal service (Arabic).
bashura	change of angle in the entrance path or corridor within a 'bent entrance' gate complex (Arabic).
bossing	style of masonry in which the outer face has a raised and roughened surface but with a smooth edging around the raised part.
burj	tower (Arabic).
caravansarai	building or complex of buildings offering shelter to merchant caravans or other travellers, sometimes fortified (from Farsi, *karwan saray* 'caravan palace').
dar al-imara	government headquarters, usually provincial or regional and often fortified (Arabic).
diwan	government ministry, or hall in which official business is conducted (Arabic).
diz	fortress or fortified city (Farsi).
fasil	area enclosed by a low wall ahead of the main defences (Arabic).
freestone	suitable pieces of rock which need minimal shaping
hamam	bath complex (Arabic).
hisba	guarding, calling to arms (Arabic).
hisn	specifically military and fortified structure (Arabic).
iwan	tall vaulted chamber, usually open at one end (Arabic and Farsi).
jisr	bridge (Arabic).
kala	castle (Turkish, from Arabic *qal'a*).
kfar	village or hamlet (Arabic).
khalij	canal (Arabic).
khandaq	ditch or moat (Arabic).
khanqah	'convent', sometimes referring to barracks for religiously motivated volunteers (Arabic).
khawabi	large ceramic containers to store drinking water (Arabic).
kuhandiz	citadel (Farsi).
madina	main part of a town or city (Arabic).
manazir	watchtower (Arabic).
manjaniqin	corps of *manjaniq* siege machine operators (Arabic).
markaz	way-stations for the *barid* government postal service (Arabic).
maydan	open area for military parades and cavalry training (Arabic).
mintar	watchtower (Arabic).
murabitin	those serving in or garrisoning a *ribat* (Arabic).
nafir	alarm (Arabic).
pakhsa	large building blocks made of earth and straw (Central Asian Turkish).
pise	rammed earth or puddled clay as a form of architectural construction.
qal'a	castle (Arabic).
qasr	high status building but not necessarily fortified (Arabic).
qubbah	dome or domed building or structure (Arabic).
rabid	outer town or suburb (Arabic).
ribat	frontier or coastal location garrisoned for defence, usually fortified, later also used for a caravansarai (Arabic).
rustication	style of masonry in which the outer face has a raised and roughened surface but without the smooth edging strip of *bossed* masonry.
sadd	barrier, dam or fortified 'long wall' (Farsi from Arabic *sudd*).
shahristan	central town of a *shahr* district, or the main part of a town or city, usually fortified (Farsi).
shaqif	cave-refuge (Arabic).
shurafat	battlements (Arabic).
shurtah	security troops, police (Arabic).
suq	specific and clearly defined market or commercial area of an Islamic town (Arabic).
sur	fortified circuit wall of a town or other enclosed area (Arabic).
thughur	frontier provinces under military administration (Arabic).
tin	clay, as used in building (Arabic).
wali	provincial governor (Arabic).
zardkhanah	weapons store (Arabic and Farsi).
zawiyah	'house of spiritual refuge', sometimes referring to barracks for religiously motivated volunteers (Arabic).

CONTENTS

INTRODUCTION   4

DESIGN AND DEVELOPMENT   9
Egypt and Syria before the Seljuks . The Great Seljuks and their rivals
Atabegs and the Seljuks' successors . Anatolian Seljuks and Ayyubids
The Mamluks . The Mongols and after . Islamic India

THE LIVING SITES   30
Egypt and Syria before the Seljuks . Seljuks and Atabegs
The Ayyubids . Mamluks, Mongols and Timurids

THE SITES AT WAR   41
The Middle East before the Seljuks . The Great Seljuks . Ayyubids and Mamluks
The Mongols and after

AFTERMATH   56

BIBLIOGRAPHY   61

INDEX   64

SARACEN STRONGHOLDS 1100–1500
THE CENTRAL AND EASTERN ISLAMIC LANDS

INTRODUCTION

The medieval walls of the port-city of Qalhat were of simple construction, with inner and outer skins of roughly trimmed field-stone, a loose rubble core and small, widely spaced towers. (Dionisius Agius)

To interpret the fortifications erected by a particular culture, its political as well as military circumstances need to be understood. For example, the idea that the later medieval Islamic world was dominated by despotic foreign rulers – usually Turks – who dominated the great cities by military force is greatly exaggerated, as is the supposed weakness of local urban and rural elites. In reality these groups shared power and responsibility, largely because the efforts of foreign military rulers to undermine the long-established power of local tribes, clans, families and households were never entirely successful. Another feature which distinguished the medieval Islamic realms from those of medieval Europe was that Muslim rulers rarely had anything like a 'divine right' to rule. Instead, they had to negotiate with existing secular, religious, economic and even military elites while their positions of authority depended upon administrative and military effectiveness, and respect for Islamic religious values.

The power and influence of women was also much greater than is generally realized, particularly within military households and those of Turkish origin. Such powerful women were, in fact, notable patrons of architecture while the cost, and thus the prestige, of major public works fell on a remarkable variety of people, both male and female. Most of the new, largely Turkish and almost invariably Turkish-influenced ruling classes were strict military heirarchies, maintained in power by troops who were divided into ethnic groups with differing prestige and even legal status, of free or unfree origin. Membership of such a military group became virtually the only path to political power for a new dynasty, and perhaps inevitably the new ruling class developed something of a fortress mentality in relation to their own subjects. This was reinforced by persistent ethnic and linguistic separation between the ruling elite and the bulk of the population (Rabbat 2006, pp. 85–86).

Directly linked to these new political and military structures was what has been described as a 'militarization of taste'. The new and largely Turkish ruling class did not start the process, however, which could already be seen during the 11th century (see *Fortress 76: Saracen Strongholds AD 630–1050*). Furthermore these new rulers, unlike their predecessors, tended to live in genuinely fortified citadels that also contained barracks, stables and parade grounds as well as administrative facilities. Paradoxically, the Mamluk sultans who ruled Egypt and Syria between 1260 and 1517 saw a reversal to an earlier aesthetic dominated by civilian, religious and even mercantile values – though in a new form.

Each region responded in a slightly different way to these political, military and cultural developments. In Egypt, during

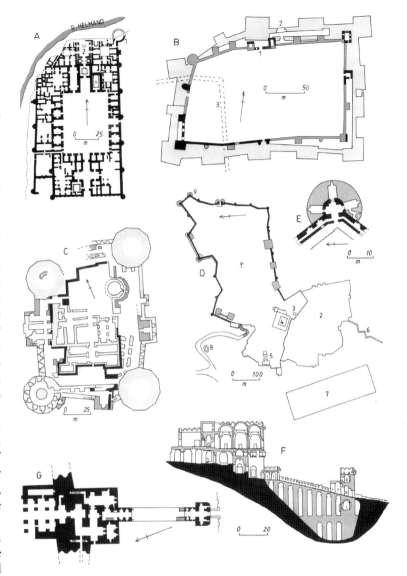

Palaces and large urban citadels.

A Lashkari Bazar, the late 11th to 12th century fortified palace built for the Ghaznawid rulers of Afghanistan and northern India. Part of the north-western corner of the palace has been eroded by the River Helmand and there was an irrigation canal in the narrow space between the palace and the river. **1** Great north-eastern tower; **2** Audience hall decorated with wall-paintings and with a small pool fed by an eastwest channel. (After Schlumberger and Ettinghausen)

B Damascus Citadel. Surviving late 11th- to late 12th-century fortress is shown in black, those existing only as foundations and the presumed line of missing parts are shown in dark grey. The 13th-century Ayyubid and Mamluk citadel is shown in light grey. **1** Bab al-Hadid 'Iron Gate'; **2** Northern gate of later citadel; **3** Underground Nahr al-Qulayt canal, entering from west and leaving to south. (After Hanisch)

C Harran Citadel. Ancient structures, including a Sabaean Temple which remained in use throughout the early Islamic period, are shown in black. Early Islamic fortifications, including the

east gate with its carved decorations, are shown in dark grey. Early 13th-century citadel is shown in light grey. (After Hanisch and Faucherre)

D Cairo Citadel; fortifications and main internal structures in the late 12th to 14th centuries. Saladin's late 12th-century fortifications in black, early 13th-century 'great towers' in grey. **1** Upper enclosure; **2** Lower enclosure; **3** Bir Yusuf well; **4** Mosque of al-Nasir Muhammad; **5** Great Iwan 'reception hall' of al-Nasir Muhammad; **6** Aqueduct from Nile; **7** *Maydan* training ground; **8** *Tablakhanah*; **9** Burj al-Ramlah tower. (After Creswell, Behrens and Rabbat)

E The north-eastern Burj al-Ramlah tower of Cairo Citadel with Saladin's late 12th-century towers in black and al-'Adil's 13th-century 'great tower' in grey. (After Creswell)

F Vertical section through the entrance complex of Aleppo Citadel. The domed upper chambers above the 13th-century inner gate were added in the late Mamluk period. (After Kennedy and Tabaa)

G Ground-floor plan of the entrance complex of Aleppo Citadel. (After Kennedy and Tabaa)

The Middle Eastern heartlands

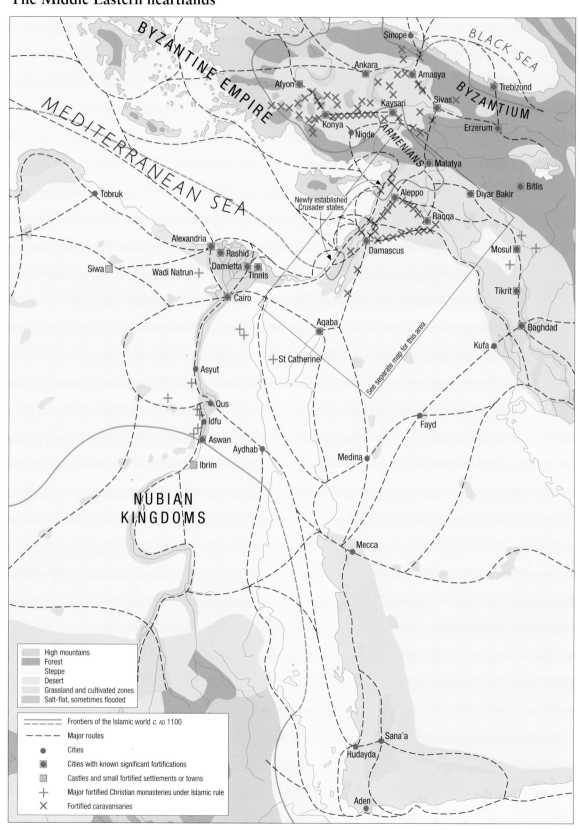

BYZANTINE EMPIRE

BYZANTIUM

BLACK SEA

MEDITERRANEAN SEA

ARMENIANS

Sinope

Ankara

Amasya

Afyon

Trebizond

Kaysari

Sivas

Konya

Erzerum

Nigde

Malatya

Bitlis

Tobruk

Aleppo

Diyar Bakir

Newly established
Crusader states

Raqqa

Mosul

Alexandria

Damascus

Rashid

Tikrit

Siwa

Damietta

Wadi Natrun

Tinnis

Cairo

Baghdad

Aqaba

Kufa

St Catherine

See separate map for this area

Asyut

Fayd

Qus

Idfu

Aswan

Aydhab

Medina

Ibrim

NUBIAN
KINGDOMS

Mecca

Hudayda

Sana'a

Aden

High mountains
Forest
Steppe
Desert
Grassland and cultivated zones
Salt-flat, sometimes flooded

Frontiers of the Islamic world *c.* AD 1100

Major routes

Cities

Cities with known significant fortifications

Castles and small fortified settlements or towns

Major fortified Christian monasteries under Islamic rule

Fortified caravansaries

Detailed map of the central Middle East

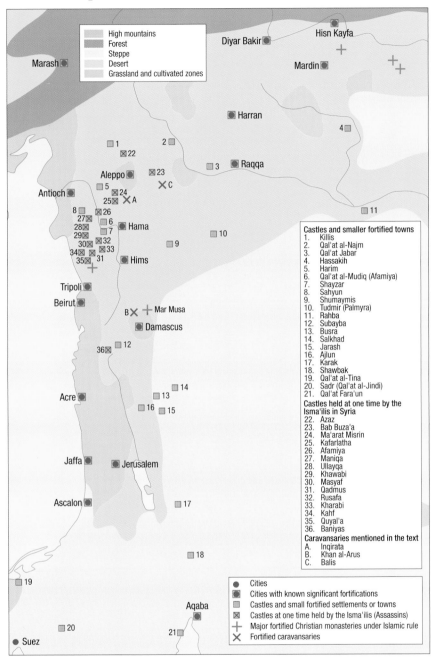

Legend (map key):

High mountains
Forest
Steppe
Desert
Grassland and cultivated zones

Castles and smaller fortified towns
1. Killis
2. Qal'at al-Najm
3. Qal'at Jabar
4. Hassakih
5. Harim
6. Qal'at al-Mudiq (Afamiya)
7. Shayzar
8. Sahyun
9. Shumaymis
10. Tudmir (Palmyra)
11. Rahba
12. Subayba
13. Busra
14. Salkhad
15. Jarash
16. Ajlun
17. Karak
18. Shawbak
19. Qal'at al-Tina
20. Sadr (Qal'at al-Jindi)
21. Qal'at Fara'un

Castles held at one time by the Isma'ilis in Syria
22. Azaz
23. Bab Buza'a
24. Ma'arat Misrin
25. Kafarlatha
26. Afamiya
27. Maniqa
28. Ullayqa
29. Khawabi
30. Masyaf
31. Qadmus
32. Rusafa
33. Kharabi
34. Kahf
35. Quyal'a
36. Baniyas

Caravansaries mentioned in the text
A. Inqirata
B. Khan al-Arus
C. Balis

● Cities
◉ Cities with known significant fortifications
□ Castles and small fortified settlements or towns
⊠ Castles at one time held by the Isma'ilis (Assassins)
+ Major fortified Christian monasteries under Islamic rule
✕ Fortified caravansaries

the second half of the 11th and most of the 12th centuries, the long-established Fatimid caliphate changed from an old-style Islamic theocracy into a military dictatorship under *wazirs* (chief ministers) whose power usually rested upon regiments recruited from the same linguistic origins as themselves. For example, *wazirs* of Armenian origin, known as the Jamalids, relied upon Armenian troops who were themselves mostly Christian; these regiments were quartered just north of the Fatimid palace city of al-Qahira (Cairo), outside the great Bab al-Futuh and Bab al-Nasr gates which had been built by the first Jamalid *wazir*, Badr al-Jamali, between 1087 and 1091. It is also important to note that Badr

7

al-Jamali's new fortifications were in response to the Seljuk Turkish threat, not that of the crusaders, who only appeared on the scene a decade later.

The situation in Syria was more complex, and even before the Seljuk Turks invaded the region the declining military power of the Fatimid caliphate led to the refortification of Jerusalem in the mid-11th century. In 1089 the Fatimid *wazir* Badr al-Jamali retook Acre and the other coastal cities from the Seljuks. These outposts remained in Fatimid hands for some years even after the First Crusade conquered the hinterland. Further north the Nusayri Mountains, facing what is now the Syrian coast, were densely populated during the Middle Ages and had been, as they still are, home to a remarkable variety of religious minorities, both Muslim and Christian. Several of the castles that were taken over by the Isma'ilis (the so-called 'Assassins') in the 12th century had already played a significant role during the 11th-century struggles between Byzantines and Arabs.

Even before the battle of Manzikirt in 1071, Byzantine power was declining in the borderlands of northern Syria. The Byzantine empire even agreed to demolish some of its newest castles in the 1060s in the hope of maintaining good relations with neighbouring Arab leaders. To the east, in the Euphrates Valley, the fluid and complicated political and military situation in the second half of the 11th century resulted in a number of fortifications which remain difficult to interpret. Here some of the last Arab rulers apparently felt a need for fortresses, as they also did in western Syria.

At the eastern end of the Jazira region, known to the ancient world as Mesopotamia, the early Islamic fortifications of the city of Mosul had seemingly been regarded as unnecessary until they were rebuilt during the local Uqaylid rulers' struggles against the invading Seljuks in 1081–82. The situation in what is now central and southern Iraq and western Iran was again different. Baghdad, the seat of an 'Abbasid caliphate which no longer exercised temporal power, may have been reduced to one-tenth of its previous population and extent.

Meanwhile most Iranian cities still had fortifications dating from the previous period, some of which had been updated in the face of more recent threats, most notably from the Seljuk Turks. The latter were Muslim, at least superficially, even before they conquered the old Islamic heartlands of Iran and the Middle East. Yet they stemmed from a pre-Islamic, Turkish, Central Asian civilization which had its own traditions of urban and military architecture, including fortified towns, caravansarais and isolated castles, especially along the caravan trade routes which are now generally referred to as the 'Silk Routes'.

DESIGN AND DEVELOPMENT

Egypt and Syria before the Seljuks

The most widespread building material in early Islamic Egypt had been brick, with very few of even the most important structures being made of stone. In greater Syria the situation was more varied; regions with suitable building stone used what was locally available for important fortified structures. In many areas this meant exceptionally hard, almost black, volcanic basalt, which was difficult to work. The resulting fortifications can therefore look grim because of their forbidding colour, rough edges and lack of decoration.

During the building boom of the mid-7th to mid-8th century, when Damascus was capital of the vast Umayyad caliphate, the expanding urban area overflowed the city's ancient defences in several directions. Some time later the massive Roman walls and gates were largely replaced by seemingly unimpressive mud-brick fortifications, parts of which were still in use during the Second Crusade's unsuccessful siege of Damascus in 1148.

Similarly, Bilbays, on the border between the Nile Delta and the desert, had only a low, mud-brick wall and no moat in 1164. Not far away, the brick fortifications of Tinnis had no fewer than 19 gates when this island-port was abandoned in the later 12th century. However, the triumph of stone over brick in high status Egyptian Islamic architecture and fortification started with the Muslim–Armenian *wazir* Badr al-Jamali, whose most famous buildings are the three great gates of Cairo: Bab al-Nasr, Bab al-Futuh and Bab Zuwailah. Whether there is much truth in the story that he had Armenian architects design these gates is unclear.

Cairo would not have a true citadel until Saladin took over in the later 12th century, whereas Damascus had its first citadel some 80 years earlier. Quite what already existed in the north-western corner of the ancient city during the second half of the 11th century is unclear, but it did include the Bab al-Hadid 'Iron Gate' and a tower called the Burj Bab al-Hadid, which seems to have been a significant defensive feature. The old *dar al-imara* or *qasr* seat of government may also have been in the same area as the present citadel.

As in all fortifications, those of the medieval Islamic world consisted of three main elements: walls, towers and gates. The circuit wall was called a *sur* in Arabic and some of the earliest well-preserved examples are next to Badr al-Jamali's gates of Cairo. On the northern side of the city they have a walkway 3.14m wide behind a crenellated parapet 48cm thick, and there is also a latrine on brackets over the outer side of this curtain. The second main element was the *burj* or tower. This remained central to Islamic military architecture, but

---

A   **NEXT PAGE: THE BAB-AL NASR IN CAIRO AT THE END OF THE 11TH CENTURY**

The Bab al-Nasr was one of three great fortified entrances of the Fatimid caliphal city of al-Qahira (Cairo), built between 1087 and 1092 to replace the earlier brick defences. Each was different, though there are close similarities between the Bab al-Futuh and the Bab Zuwailah. The decorative cavalry *turs* and elongated infantry *januwiya* shields on the Bab al-Nasr (shown as insets, **A**) had a symbolic purpose that is no longer understood. The simple, straight-through entrance (shown in ground-floor plan **B1**, and first-floor and wall-walk plan **B2**) was defended by machicolations and arrow slits, while slots in the platform may have been anchorage points for a mangonel. Later written evidence also indicates that there was a *bashura* 'bent entrance' in front of the gate (shown in dotted lines on the main image), though its construction date is unknown and nothing remains today. Also shown is a sectional plan of the staircase-tower behind the eastern gate-tower (**C**). To the right of the Bab al-Nasr was an overhanging latrine on the curtain wall (**D**), beyond which was the first of the rectangular defensive towers (**E**). A massive Fatimid tower enclosed the northern minaret of the earlier Mosque of al-Hakim (**F**), the lower part of which still exists inside the tower; the upper part, which was later rebuilt, has here been replaced by a surviving Fatimid minaret at Isna in southern Egypt. In the lower right is a plan of late-11th century fortifications at the eastern end of the north wall of Cairo: **1**, Bab al-Nasr; **2**, first intermediary tower; **3**, second intermediary tower; **4**, 'Minaret Tower; **5**, Bab al-Futuh.

F

B1

B2

C

D

E

1   2   3   4   5

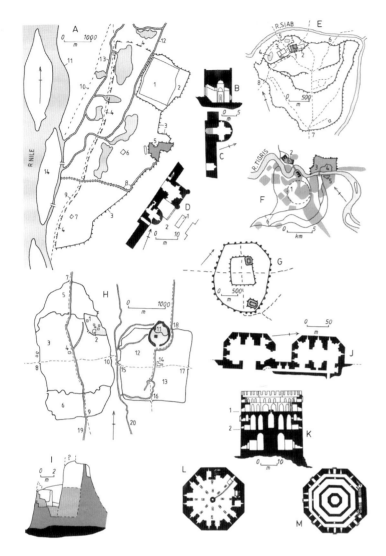

tended to become substantially larger and stronger from the early years of the 13th century onwards. The final main element was the *bab* or gate. Having advanced the northern and southern walls of the Fatimid palace-city of Cairo in 1087 and 1092 respectively, Badr al-Jamali's architects built three new gates. Despite the presence of centuries-old knowledge of how to construct a *bashura* or bent-entrance, all three are 'straight through' gates; the very deep-set doors were protected by arrow-slits and missile-dropping apertures to the sides and above. Egypt's southern frontier city of Aswan had some sort of defences when besieged by Nubians and ex-Fatimid Armenian refugee soldiers in 1172, but nothing now remains other than the fortified Coptic monastery of St. Simeon, largely dating from the Fatimid and early Ayyubid 12th century.

Fortifications from the immediate pre-crusader period do survive in Syria, though most are embedded within later structures. One such site is the little-known citadel of Salkhad, which is said to have been founded or enlarged in 1073–74 by Hassan Ibn Mismar, chief of the Arab Banu Kalb

Urban fortifications.

A The medieval city of Cairo. **1** 10th-century palace-city of al-Qahira; **2** Extended walled area of the late-Fatimid caliphal city with additional fortification by Saladin; **3** Saladin's eastern urban fortifications; **4** Saladin's projected but uncompleted western fortifications; **5** Citadel; **6** Mosque of Ibn Tulun; **7** Mosque of 'Amr Ibn al-Aasi; **8** Early Mamluk aqueduct; **9** shoreline of Nile *c.* 800; **10** Shoreline of Nile *c.* 1200; **11** Shoreline since early 14th century; **12** *al-Khalij* canal to Gulf of Suez; **13** *Khalij al-Nasiri* irrigation canal; **14** Rawda Island. Seasonal or permanent *birkit* pools are shown in light grey. (After Rabbat and Creswell)

B–C Cairo; section and plan of first tower west of the early Ayyubid Burj al-Zafar in the northern city wall. (After Creswell)

D Cairo; plan of early Ayyubid Bab al-Jadid, eastern city gate. (After Creswell)

E Samarqand; late 12th and early 13th century. **1** citadel; **2** palace; **3** Great mosque; **4** Cisterns; **5** Bukhara Gate; **6** Ghaina Gate; **7** Kish Gate; **8** Naubirhar Gate. (After Buryakov, Macleod and Kaufman)

F Baghdad, 12th century. Inhabited areas are shown in dark grey. **1** Site of abandoned 'Abbasid Round City; **2** Walled palace and gardens; **3** Fortified New Baghdad; **4** Walled palace and gardens; **5–6** Irrigation canals. (After Lassner)

G Kulan; 12th and early 13th centuries. Inner fortified citadels are shown in dark grey. (After Buryakov)

H Marw; 12th century. **1** *Shahyar Ark* inner citadel of Sultan-Qal'a; **2** palace; **3** Main town of Sultan-Qal'a; **4** Mausoleum of Sultan Ahmad Sanjar; **5** Northern fortified suburb; **6** Southern fortified suburb; **7** Poi-Madgan Gate; **8** Firuz Gate; **9** Sari-Madgan Gate; **10** Shahristan Gate; **11** Ruins of Erk-Qal'a citadel; **12** Canals; **13** Largely abandoned city of Gyaurkala; **14** Mosque of Banu Mahan; **15** Rabat Gate; **16** Balic Gate; **17** Singan Gate; **18** Dermuchkan Gate; **19** Madgan canal; **20** Razik canal. (After Herrmann and Buryakov)

I Section through southern city wall of Marw from the late 11th to early 13th century. Undisturbed soil black; first wall and outer wall dark grey; the second strengthening mid-grey; the third strengthening light grey. (After Herrmann)

J Aleppo, plan of the walled city's (probably 12th-century) Bab Antakiyah. (After Sauvaget)

K Alanya, vertical section through 13th-century 'Red Tower'. **1** first floor; **2** second floor. (After Rice)

L Alanya, plan of the second floor of the 'Red Tower'. (After Rice)

M Alanya, plan of the ground floor of the 'Red Tower'. (After Rice)

tribe, as a base for attacks against what was then Fatimid-ruled Damascus. The little that was recorded about the men who designed and constructed these Fatimid-period fortresses tends to be clouded by legend. One example is al-Maqrizi's famous story about Badr al-Jamali's Cairo gates: 'They relate that three brothers, who were architects, came from al-Ruha (Edessa, now Urfa) to Cairo, and each built one of the great gates', the implication being that they were Armenians. Unfortunately, the fortification of Armenia proper, and of the emerging Armenian Kingdom of Cilicia, had remarkably little in common with those of late-Fatimid Cairo.

The Great Seljuks and their rivals

Mud-brick and fired brick had long been traditional building materials in Central Asia and parts of eastern Iran, often in the form of very large, unfired blocks of earth and straw known as *pakhsa*. This tradition was clearly used by the Seljuks as they spread their authority westwards into Iran to form the Great Seljuk sultanate. Here Yazd was already a well-fortified city with two iron or iron-clad gates, but in the mid-11th century the local ruler ordered its city wall to be rebuilt with

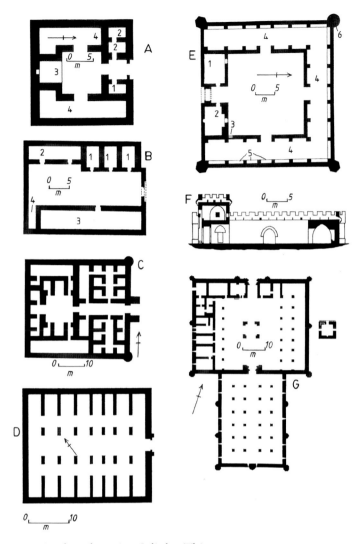

towers and four iron gates in an attempt to resist the advancing Seljuks. This was a high desert region where, according to the 13th-century Persian scholar al-Qazwini, the mud-brick structures of Yazd lasted as long as fired-bricks did elsewhere because there was so little rain. By the late medieval period Yazd was surrounded by a deep dry moat and double, or in places triple, walls crowned with machicolations.

Some cities in Islamic Central Asia and Iran had long been surrounded by fortifications of huge extent, and this tradition continued well into the 12th century. Marw-i Shahijan, or 'Great Marw', became one of the Seljuks' main military centres and consisted of several different towns developed over different periods. The one known as Sultan-Qal'a is on the western side and flourished from the Arab-Islamic conquest in the 8th century, its surrounding

ABOVE RIGHT Mercantile fortifications.
A Balis, plan of 14th-century Mamluk *barid* station. **1** Guardroom; **2** Dormitories; **3** Mosque; **4** Stables and storage areas. (After Sauvaget)
B Manakhur, plan of 14th-century Mamluk *barid* station *or khan*. **1** Dormitories; **2** Storage area; **3** Stables; **4** Latrine. (After Sauvaget)
C Tashrabat, plan of early 15th-century *khan*. (After Buryakov)

D Zivrik, plan of 13th-century Saljuq *khan*. (After Ettinghausen)
E – Inqirata, plan of 14th-century Mamluk *khan*. **1** Guardroom; **2** Mosque; **3** Stairs to upper floor; **4** Stables; **5** Mangers; **6** Latrine in north-western tower. (After Sauvaget)
F – Inqirata, vertical section of *khan*. (After Sauvaget)
G – Sultan Han, plan of 13th-century Saljuq *khan*. (After Ettinghausen)

mud-brick wall and numerous towers being rebuilt by the Great Seljuk sultan Malik Shah in the 1070s. During the 12th century Marw-i Shahijan also had inner defensive walls which separated the different quarters of the city, the resulting fortifications being considered amongst the finest in existence. The former were erected either on a clay platform or on the ruins of demolished buildings. However, the most interesting aspect of the outer fortifications was that they were hollow, presumably designed to face nomadic enemies who lacked stone-throwing weapons or other such siege machinery.

The next serious change to Marw's fortifications probably dated from the mid-12th century when the eastern part of the Great Seljuk realm was threatened by Qarakhanids and Khwarazmshahs, both of whom had armies equipped for siege warfare (Herrmann 2001, pp. 40–41). For example, the fortifications of the suburbs around Sultan-Qal'a probably date from the reign of Sultan Sanjar, consisting of circuit walls and towers which protruded only a short distance from the walls. There may also have been a moat, though this remains unconfirmed.

There were similarly impressive urban defences further west and east, Qazwin having a double fortification and an outer wall with 206 towers, while Harat similarly had a double wall with 149 towers. Under Seljuk rule the curtain wall of Isfahan was said to be 3.5 *farsakhs* (approx. 21km) in circumference while the urban quarters were separated by gates, presumably through inner walls.

The main gate of Saladin's desert castle of Sadr (Qal'at al-Gindi) was decorated with a pair of carved shields and swords on each side of a dedicatory inscription. (Author's photograph)

Three eastern Islamic citadel-palaces of this period have been studied in detail: Tirmidh (Termez) dating from *c.* 1030, Lashkar-i Bazar from the later 11th to early 13th century, and Ghazna from the 12th century. The best preserved is Lashkar-i Bazar which covers an area of 100 x 250m. It is within the same traditions as earlier Islamic fortified palace-compounds, with a central courtyard, an elaborate entrance complex, and a tall open-fronted *iwan* arched audience area and dome facing the entrance. Another superb *iwan* faced the River Helmand while self-contained dwelling units facing the courtyard recalled the earlier Umayyad so-called 'desert palace' of Qasr al-Hayr al-Sharqi in Syria. The internal structures are largely built of mud-brick on foundations of fired-brick, with fired-brick also used for the main load-bearing elements. The surrounding fortifications are also mostly of mud-brick, all the towers being solid except for a much larger tower at the north-eastern corner. Water was channelled to the highly decorated main audience hall having presumably been raised from the canal next to the Helmand River (Schlumberger 1952, pp. 251–70).

Intensive study of the Sultan Qal'a at Marw-i Shahijan provides further information about mud-brick fortifications, the town wall being defended by towers spaced 28m apart and projecting 3m from walls which were themselves at least 5.5m wide. There was almost certainly a walkway

ABOVE LEFT
The carving on the early 12th-century Bab Talisman in Baghdad was of the highest quality. Unfortunately, it was destroyed by an accidental explosion in 1917. (Staatliche Museen Berlin)

ABOVE RIGHT
Agzikarahan is one of the best-preserved fortified khans in Turkey. In the centre of its courtyard was a raised *musallah* prayer room. (Author's photograph)

on top, accessed by L-shaped staircases 70cm wide and at least 4m long. Galleries and chambers within the curtain wall had arrow slits, which also provided ventilation and light. The upper fighting platform and some parts of its battlements survive, the latter being pierced by arrow slits between decorative pillars. A section through the defences also exposes the surprisingly thin parapet battlements of an earlier wall enclosed inside the later one.

In places the original main mud-brick wall was hollow with arrow-slits which, though well built and elegant, were not strong enough to withstand an attack by stone-throwing artillery. When Sultan Qal'a was attacked, these hollow walls were so severely damaged that, instead of being repaired, they and the arrow-slits were filled with mud-brick and rubble. The platform on which the fortifications were erected was also levelled and extended to allow the construction of a secondary line of defence, or *fausse-braie*, which was 5m high on the southern side of Sultan Qal'a. Here a raised, plaster-covered floor of mud-brick and *pakhsa* formed a fighting platform in front of the main defences. A second and then a third such *fausse-braie* was eventually constructed before the fortifications were finally abandoned (Herrmann 2001, pp. 34–35).

Few of the isolated castles which dot Iran have caught the imagination of westerners more than those associated with the Isma'ilis. Their design philosophy did not rely on great citadels or man-made heights. Instead, in the words of the leading specialist in their history, Peter Willey:

> The Ismailis, wherever possible, built upon the crown of a great rock or mountain, dividing the fortifications up into self-contained sections, culminating in the citadel at the top. The best example of this is Qa'in … The Ismaili concept was much more sophisticated too as provision had to be made for ample water storage. (Willey 2005, p. 97)

Many Isma'ili outposts remained unrecognized until modern times, especially in northern and eastern Iran. Furthermore, Willey notes, the so-called 'Assassin castles' were more than mere military strongpoints, serving as administrative and cultural centres.

In each case the Isma'ilis only took control of strongholds in areas which they believed they could defend, usually in remote and difficult terrain. At the same time the fortresses had to be capable of maintaining efficient communications using fire and smoke beacons or other methods. Furthermore, the area had to have raw materials to build or repair fortresses, as well as a workforce and food supplies. In other words the terrain needed to be both difficult and defensible, yet also self-sufficient and with sufficient local support for the Isma'ili cause. Virtually all Isma'ili castles were in locations out of range of existing siege artillery, either because of the steepness of the approach or the lack of nearby hills. Moreover, most of their walls were almost impossible for siege engineers to undermine, again because of a steep slope or solid rock foundations. Alamut was the most famous of these 'Assassin castles' and served as a sort of Isma'ili capital. Here the existing Dailamite castle was greatly extended, being divided into an inner castle and various outworks to which further buildings were later added on the south-eastern side.

Other isolated castles in Iran have received less attention. Most of those situated on top of mountains followed the contours of their location, while those on lower hills tended to be rectangular. However, a well-preserved castle near Jajarm between Astarabad (now Gorgan) and Sabzarai is hexagonal with a tower at each corner. Though attributed to the last Khwarazmshah, Jalal al-Din (1220–31), its design suggests a later medieval date.

The castles of what are now eastern Turkey, western Iran and the Caucasus states were very varied, this having long been a wartorn frontier region between Graeco-Roman and Persian civilizations, and then between Christendom and Islam. One of the most distinctive is Oltu Kalesi in north-east Turkey. Quite when it was first built is unknown, but the castle was taken by the Seljuk Turks in the 1070s and subsequently disputed between Muslim Turks and Christian Georgians until the 15th century. Its walls follow the roughly triangular rocky outcrop on which it is built, and are strengthened by salient corner towers, the largest of which appears to be solid except for a corridor within its northern flank. Otherwise its complicated entrance, massive salients, plan adopted to the outcrop, battered (sloping) walls and avoidance of sharp exterior corners were typical of earlier Armenian fortifications in these regions (Edwards 1985, pp. 18–19).

Other buildings could also be fortified or could serve a military purpose. For example, the *khanqah* complex of religious buildings attributed to Jamal al-Din at Anau in Central Asia was clearly intended to be defensible. Another example of a fortified *khanqah* is that of Pir Sadat near Baku on the Caspian Sea, which became a popular pilgrimage centre. The complex consists of an irregular, four-sided, fortified enclosure with round corner towers, semi-circular intermediary towers in three walls and a rectangular fortified gateway in the fourth. Inside this 'religious fortress' were a ceremonial hall, library, refectory and kitchen, plus guestrooms, sleeping cells for the *sufi* Islamic mystics and finer quarters for their *shaykh* (Harrison 2004, p. 233).

Less obviously military were the exceptionally tall, often decorated, free-standing *manarah* minarets built from the later 11th to 13th century in Azarbaijan, Iran and some

The massive portal of Timur-i Lang's brick-built Ak-Serai palace within the citadel of Kish (now Shakhrisabz) was almost entirely covered by glazed brick geometric mosaics and inscriptions in green, blue and gold.

regions further east. These can still be seen at Baku, Isfahan, Bukhara, Ghazna and Jam. Their purpose is not entirely clear and, while they could certainly be used to call the faithful to prayer, they may equally have been expressions of piety, power or have served as victory monuments. Some in northern Iran and Central Asia may have contained lights to guide travellers, while many are also located in strategic positions where they could serve as defensive observation posts.

Little is known about builders and architects from the Seljuk period. Where the Isma'ilis are concerned, however, it is certain that their leaders and senior men travelled very widely.

Atabegs and the Seljuks' successors

The fragmentation of the Great Seljuk sultanate was followed by a period of intensive military building. The architectural styles and materials did not change much, though many old brick fortifications were replaced by stone, as at Jazirat Ibn Umar at the northern limit of commercial navigation on the River Tigris. To the south, near the River Euphrates, the castle of Rahba was repaired and strengthened several times, the work dating from the 12th-century period of Nur al-Din combining traditional brick and stone. Far away in Oman, the Indian Ocean port of Qalhat had an extensive but crude city wall whose outer and inner surfaces were of uncut freestone with an infill of rubble, plus small, widely spaced rectangular towers.

The restored enclosure wall and new gate complex which turned the Temple of Bel at Palmyra into a fortress in the 12th century was made of masonry taken from the surrounding Roman ruins, though this was roughly dressed in the same style as seen in Damascus during this period (Allen 1996). However, it is important to note that while fine bossed masonry was rarely if ever used in the Middle East from Roman to crusader times, simpler rusticated masonry was; both offered the same military advantages by denying a flat or regular surface to an attacker's siege machines. Meanwhile, the huge enclosed spaces which had characterized some fortified Central Asian cities now appeared in parts of the Middle East, though the idea that these were used to grow food for a garrison and inhabitants in time of siege appears impractical.

Baghdad, while still very important, had shrunk considerably by the second half of the 11th century and now consisted of separated urban areas, the most important being on the eastern bank of the Tigris, around the caliphal and other palaces. According to the traveller Ibn Jubayr, Baghdad had 17 separate quarters in the 12th century, each with from two to eight *hamam* public baths, so this was clearly still a substantial and flourishing city. Caliphal palace-complexes covered a quarter of *Sharqiyya* or eastern Baghdad, which was now the most important part of the city, but even this does not seem to have been walled until after the river overflowed in 1070, causing considerable damage. So the fortifications built by Caliph al-Mustazhir in 1095 could be seen as flood defences as much as military ones. They were rebuilt by Caliph al-Mustarshid in 1123 with four brick gates and a mud-brick wall 22 'arm's lengths' wide. It was breached again in 1159, so a proper flood-defence dyke was erected around the fortifications.

Mosul was now almost as important as Baghdad, its fortifications having at least 11 fortified gates during the 12th century. Again according to Ibn Jubayr, it was protected by two walls containing covered 'firing chambers' and with many closely spaced towers. Much more remains of Aleppo's medieval defences, most notably the citadel. Nur al-Din (1147–74) added an

The largely 15th-century Upper Citadel of Harat was built of brick on a rocky outcrop, with large towers with a pronounced batter or slope, linked by high walls with internal shooting galleries near the top. (Geza Fehervari)

outwork or *fasil* to the city's existing curtain wall to join the already fortified but separate south-eastern suburb of Qal'at al-Sharif to the main city defences. Nur al-Din's work also included a second circuit wall or *sur* in advance of the main city wall (Allen 1996).

From the late 11th to mid-12th centuries Damascus enjoyed a period of prosperity, despite the political and military turmoil. As a result suburbs developed on the northern and south-western sides of the existing walls and gates. Significant damage was caused by an earthquake in 1140 and the subsequent hurried repairs to several towers and lengths of wall sometimes used masonry from ancient cemeteries. This may also have been when some existing, roughly built, half-round towers were erected on top of more formidable rectangular foundations. Looking at parts of the recently cleared southern city wall might suggest that replacement of the old mud-brick defences by stone may simply have involved replacing what was already built on top of the massive masonry foundations of the ancient walls (Braune 1999).

B   SECTION THROUGH THE 'TEMPLE' CASTLE AT BAALBAK, MID-13TH CENTURY

The early Byzantines built a basilica church in front of the large Temple of Jupiter overlooking Baalbak in Lebanon. The pagan temple platform was then used as a fortress early in the Islamic period, but this entailed little more than closing most entrances and strengthening the outer walls. However, with the creation of the Crusader States, Baalbak became a strategic frontier position. Its defences were strengthened by Najm al-Din Ayyub in 1139 and following an earthquake in 1170, which apparently caused the south-western corner of the temple platform to collapse, Nur al-Din repaired this 'temple citadel'. During the subsequent Ayyubid period the abandoned Christian basilica was replaced by a palace, next to which was a large water cistern – insecure water supplies being the fortress's main weakness. Early in the 13th century the local Ayyubid ruler, al-Malik al-Amjad Bahramshah, extended the fortified palace across the collapsed south-western corner, adding a mosque and an entrance complex, and probably made the smaller Temple of Bacchus into a significant strongpoint. The large southern tower was probably also part of Bahramshah's

fortifications. The inset plan shows the Citadel of Baalbak in the mid-13th century.

A   Temple of Bacchus converted into a donjon or keep.
B   Covered passageway between Bahramshah's palace-citadel and the cistern.
C   Mosque.
D   Man-powered mangonel on the roof of the mosque.
E   South-western tower of the citadel.
F   Western wall of the citadel.
G   Moat.
H   Temple of Jupiter.
I   North-western tower.
J   North-eastern tower.
K   South-eastern tower.

Plan of the palace of the Citadel of Baalbak in the mid-13th century:
Graeco-Roman construction is in brown.
Early Byzantine construction is in orange.
Medieval Islamic construction is in blue.

Section through the 'Temple' castle at Baalbak, mid-13th century

The 12th century 'Maiden Tower' of the port-city of Baku was once on the shoreline of the Caspian Sea. Designed by an architect named Mas'ud Ibn Da'ud, its striped masonry seems to have been characteristic of this part of the Caucasus. (Angus Hay)

Darband (Derbent) on the western shore of the Caspian Sea was in a different situation. Known to the Arabs as 'The Gate of Gates' and to the Turks as the 'The Iron Gates', it was said to have been fortified by the Sassanian King of Kings Anushirwan in the 6th century AD, his wall being seven *farsakhs* (over 40km) long and stretching from the mountains to the sea. Even today the remains of a fortification run from the coast to the Kara Syrt River. In the 10th century, when Darband was the main port on the Caspian, it had a narrow harbour between two sea walls that could be closed by a chain. Under Seljuk rule from the 11th century, it developed into a thriving Islamic town which, according to al-Qazwini in 1275, was about two-thirds of a *farsakh* (almost 4km) long but only a bowshot wide, protected by a wall, one end of which was washed by the Caspian Sea. A tower in this city wall also contained a mosque to serve the local population. Because of their exposed but strategically vital position, the fortifications of Darband were constantly manned by troops who also kept a warning beacon-fire on an adjoining mountaintop in readiness.

Friar William of Rubruck, recounting his journey to the court of the Mongol Khan Möngke in 1253–55 was similarly impressed by Darband:

> The longitude of the city covers more than a mile, and on the mountain peak there is a strong fortress; in latitude, however, it is only a large stone's throw. It possesses very stout walls, though no moats, and towers made of large polished stones; but the Tartars have demolished the upper parts of the towers and the buttresses [*propugnacula murorum*], reducing the towers to the level of the wall.

During this period local rulers mostly took up residence in urban fortresses, so that palace and citadel virtually become one and the same. At first, however, they often made use of existing suitable buildings, such as the huge Roman theatre at Busra. The first identifiable additional fortifications there date from 1089 when the local governor Kumushtekin extended the towers that flanked the stage. The next significant work was by Altuntash, a local governor of Armenian origin who unsuccessfully sought independence; he added a large new tower made of a mixture of smooth and bossed masonry. Altuntash also closed the other ground-floor entrances of the theatre, with the exception of those that were narrowed for use as military posterns (Yovitchich 2004, pp. 207–08).

The sacred precinct and Graeco-Roman temples at Baalbak had been used as a refuge for centuries, yet the first identifiable Islamic work from the first half of the 12th century merely comprised walling up gates and porticos to transform the walls of the temple platform into a citadel (Van Ess 1998, p. 58). 'Imad al-Din Zangi and his successor Nur al-Din next transformed the upper part of these walls with covered walkways, loopholes and machicolations. Following a severe earthquake in 1170, when the south-western corner of the sacred platform probably collapsed, this area was rebuilt as a strong castle with an integral mosque and other palatial or administrative structures next to the Temple of Bacchus, which was itself converted into a keep topped by a crenellated wall.

Damascus contained no natural features that lent themselves to the construction of a citadel, so the north-western corner of the roughly rectangular old city was probably chosen because it was partly defended by the River Barada and Nahr Aqrabani Canal, and may already have been the site of the *dar al-imara* or centre of local government. It also controlled the Nahr Banyas Canal, which, with the Nahr Qanawat slightly further south, brought drinking water into the city. There appear to have been four phases of construction before the entire citadel of Damascus was surrounded by massive new fortifications during the early 13th century. The original, late 11th-century Seljuk citadel enclosed an area of about 210 × 130m, some 600m of the wall still surviving inside later walls and towers, though only a little of this is Seljuk. Most of it comprises 12th-century repairs or strengthening.

Until the introduction of much larger urban towers, there seem to have been few changes in the design of urban defences. For example, the large round corner towers of the city of Diyar Bakir in south-eastern Turkey date from the very early 13th century. Two in particular, called the Ulu Badan and the Yedi Kardash, are over 25m in diameter and were constructed for the Artuqid ruler al-Salih Nasir al-Din Mahmud (1201–22/23). There was, perhaps, more variety where gates were concerned. In Baghdad the gate towers of the later city walls are built of fired-brick, with stone used for some important elements and for decoration. They were sited on the far side of bridges across the surrounding moats and both the surviving Bab al-Wastani and the well-recorded Bab Talisman incorporated *bashura* bent entrances.

The fortress of Qal'at Jabar largely dates from the 12th century, and the sophistication of its main defensive towers has been brutally exposed by the ravages of earthquake and war. (Author's photograph)

Even at the time of the Second Crusade the gates of Damascus still lacked some of the sophisticated elements of fortification already seen in other great Islamic cities. There were, for example, no integral *bashura* bent entrance gates, though something comparable would be added outside the Bab Sharqi, probably by Nur al-Din, in the second half of the 12th century. Here the southern and central arches of the old Roman triple-gate were blocked, leaving only the northern one clear, while a separate bent entrance structure was added in front of this remaining entrance.

Anatolian Seljuks and Ayyubids

The ex-Byzantine eastern provinces of Anatolia, in what is now Turkey, were already highly fortified areas when they fell to the Turks in the late 11th century. As a result the Seljuk Turkish rulers of what became the Sultanate of Rum and their Danishmandid Turkish rivals did not need to build much more. As the political and strategic situation changed in the later 13th century a number of relatively small castles were constructed while urban fortifications were upgraded or strengthened. However, this process is best seen as the background to the development of Ottoman military architecture.

The Bab al-Wastani, dating from 1123, is the only one of Baghdad's medieval gates to survive, along with a stretch of the city wall and the bridge that once crossed the moat. (Author's photograph)

Meanwhile, some distinctive types of Islamic fortified building were introduced to Anatolia, such as the Khwand Khatun complex in Kayseri. It consists of a linked mosque and *madrasa* Islamic school, both protected by crenellated walls, interval towers and round corner towers to form a unified fortified bulding (Harrison 2004, p. 234). The most distinctive Turkish fortifications of pre-Ottoman Turkey are, nevertheless, the numerous *khans* that lined the area's overland main trade routes.

The most distinctive form of architectural decoration in Seljuk Anatolia was, however, the use of external layers of plaster. This was not an entirely new concept, having long been used in Turkish Central Asia and, to a more limited degree, elsewhere in the early Islamic world. What made Turkish Anatolia different was the use of plaster over well-made stone fortifications, its functional application as a form of architectural camouflage and the further development of that idea with painted, false masonry joints.

Elsewhere in the Middle East the Ayyubid and early Mamluk periods saw a vigorous exchange of ideas with the 'Franks' or crusader settlers, especially where fortification was concerned. In some respects the Muslims surpassed their Christian rivals, but once the last crusader outpost had been retaken the urge to innovate faded. The main development in Ayyubid military architecture was improved provision for flanking fire, while there was also a tendency to adopt the massive monumentality seen in much crusader fortification. Yet this did not mean that earlier styles and materials fell out of use. For example, the north-western tower of the Ayyubid citadel at Raqqa still consisted of mud-brick with a skin of fired-brick. At Rahba, during the fifth phase of rebuilding which probably dates from this period, parts of the castle's sloping glacis were reinforced with blocks of conglomerate 'pudding stone'. The change from brick to stone seen at Rahba was also found at Azaz, where the Ayyubid ruler of Aleppo rebuilt an earlier brick citadel dating from the 10th century.

The most remarkable Ayyubid fortress is the citadel of Aleppo. Here the builders had a high, commanding eminence on which to build, but most of it was not a stable natural feature, being a great *tel* or mound of debris

C   QAL'AT 'AYLA (JAZIRAT FARA'UN), c. 1187

The Qal'at 'Ayla on Jazirat Fara'un ('Pharoah's Island') was built for Saladin shortly after he retook Aqaba from the crusader Kingdom of Jerusalem, thus earning himself prestige by 'liberating the Darb al-Hajj (Islamic Pilgrimage Road)' between Egypt and Arabia. Nevertheless, the old desert road across Sinai remained vulnerable to crusader raids, so Saladin had the route moved southwards to a more secure position while building Qal'at 'Ayla and Sadr near its eastern and western ends.

 1 Northern fortifications.
 2 Southern fortifications.
 3 Outer walls.
 4 Storage building.
 5 Western wall of the northern fortifications.
 6 Eastern wall of the northern fortifications.

 7 Main entrance to the northern fortifications.
 8 Southern entrance to the northern fortifications.
 9 Water cistern.
10 Hamam (bath-house).
11 Carrier-pigeon loft.
12 One of the external towers.
13 Mosque.
14 Entrance to presumed harbour.
15 Sinai c. 1187.
    A – the frontier between crusader and Islamic territory.
    B – traditional routes across the Sinai.
    C – new southerly route created by Saladin.
    D – the main Sinai fortresses.
16 Carved stone slab recording the building of the castle.

Qal'at 'Ayla (Jazirat Fara'un), *c.* 1187

16
8
5
9
7
1
11
13
6
14
4
10
2
3
12
15
Gaza
al-'Arish
Farama
Nahl
Suez
Sadr
Aqaba
Qal'at 'Ayla
A
B
C
D
(see key opposite)

The basic form of the Naryn Kala citadel of Darband (Derbent) seems to date from the 12th or early 13th century, though it was extensively rebuilt by the Safavid Persians in the 17th century. (Daghestan State Tourist Information Service)

resulting from millennia of human habitation. As a result there were a number of occasionally fatal collapses, sometimes as building work was in progress. The ex-Byzantine, ex-crusader fortress of Sahyun (Saone) offered a much more stable environment. Here the first Ayyubid additions and repairs were functional rather than aesthetic, the walls being made of roughly squared, medium-sized stones, with only the corners and doorjambs being of finely cut ashlar blocks, some with raised bosses. Saladin's castle on Jazirat Fara'un in the Gulf of Aqaba was even more utilitarian, with very little dressed stone and decoration.

It has been suggested that the earliest Islamic example of true bossed, as distinct from rusticated, masonry is at Ajlun castle in Jordan, in work dating from 1184. If this is correct, the Ayyubid masons almost certainly copied the style from their 'Frankish' opposite numbers. The Muslims then developed a form of pyramidal bossing with smooth, faceted sides, which made a wall look impressive but offered no additional military advantage.

The Ayyubid dynasty was responsible for a number of very impressive citadels, that of Cairo being the earliest. Here the main surviving Ayyubid military structures form part of the northern enclosure, whereas the main residential or royal structures were in the southern enclosure. The Ayyubid citadel at Harran is smaller and less well preserved. When al-'Adil was made governor in 1192 he almost immediately started to strengthen a citadel that was already a century and a half old, but at Harran, unlike Damascus, most of the old fortifications were removed rather than being enclosed, with the notable exception of the carved 11th-century gate. Al-'Adil also seems to have experimented at Harran before beginning his more important work on the citadel of Damascus, especially where the shape of the four, huge, eleven-sided corner towers was concerned. They were approximately 30m across, each differing slightly. That on the east had three stories and an open platform, while the main defensive level consisted of a corridor running parallel to the seven outward-facing sides. The upper stories were of ashlar masonry, while the missing summit of the tower was probably of brick. However, the load-bearing stresses of the eleven-sided towers could not be evenly spread because the towers themselves were asymmetrical where they faced into the citadel. This was probably why the design was not repeated at Damascus (Hanisch 2004, pp. 165–78).

In Damascus the large rectangular towers which dominated al-'Adil's virtually rebuilt citadel combined the functions of barracks and defence; their design resulted in well-lit, well-aired quarters which were separated from the noise and other activities of the citadel by a system of internal staircases. As such they remained in use almost unchanged until the 20th century (Hanisch 2004, p. 177). Al-'Adil's engineers also rebuilt the citadel's already sophisticated hydraulic systems, sometimes tunnelling anew through the bedrock beneath the fortress and laying down a complex system of large ceramic pipes and brickwork.

The great 13th-century citadel of Aleppo, built by the city's Ayyubid rulers, is now entered through a late Mamluk barbican or detached lower entry fortification on the south side of the moat, then across a viaduct and up the now revetted glacis to an upper entry complex which is deeply embedded in the citadel's steep slope. The lower part of this entry block, plus some of the viaduct, dates from the time of al-Malik al-Zahir (1186–1216), whereas its upper part was added by the Mamluks.

The Mamluks

During the second half of the 13th century, after the Mamluk sultanate had overthrown the Ayyubids, there was a big effort to restore and greatly strengthen captured crusader strongholds. This was accompanied by an increasing desire for such fortifications to overawe both friends and enemies. Meanwhile, architectural influences flowed from Damascus, as the main Syrian military centre, to Egypt throughout the later Ayyubid and early Mamluk periods, despite the fact that Cairo remained the political centre. The process was, however, reversed from the later 14th century when military architectural influences started to flow the other way, first to Damascus and then to Aleppo.

With increasing European Christian domination of the Mediterranean, significant effort was put into defending the coasts, though this did not necessarily mean the construction of major fortifications. In Egypt Sultan Baybars (1260–77) was credited with repairing the walls of Alexandria and adding a moat, as well as building a tower at Rashid (Rosetta). As European naval domination grew stronger, the beautiful fortress of Qayit Bay was erected on the site of the ancient *pharos* lighthouse of Alexandria. It was started in 1477, completed two years later, and was from the outset designed to house cannon. Towards the close of the Mamluk period the fortifications of Rashid were strengthened yet again, while some Red Sea ports were fortified for the first time. On the Syro-Palestinian coast the main crusader castle of Tripoli, which stood a short distance inland from the old port, was extensively reconstructed in 1308, after which nothing further was done until the Ottoman period, although a series of smaller towers was constructed to defend the port.

Elsewhere the focus remained on citadels, though the big changes to that of Cairo mostly concerned the internal buildings. While there seem to have been few changes to the citadel of Damascus, the citadel of Aleppo had some impressive additions, those undertaken during the late 15th and very early 16th centuries being intended to strengthen the Mamluks' northern frontier against their increasingly powerful Ottoman neighbours. Here the last major project was a magnificent throne room above the 13th-century Ayyubid gate, where the Mamluk governor Jakam min 'Iwad and other senior *amirs* personally helped by carrying stones on their backs, as witnessed by the historian Ibn Shihna when he was a boy in 1406.

The Mamluk Sultan al-Nasir restored the citadel of Jerusalem in 1310, giving it high walls, battlements and many loopholes which, according to the European pilgrim Felix Fabri who visited Jerusalem around 1480, were for siege machines as well as archers and crossbowmen. Fabri also reported that the once-deep moat was now silting up, and the part that faced into the city was being used for growing vegetables.

One area where there was significant improvement in Mamluk military architecture was the design of fortified curtain walls. Here circulation was enhanced by the construction of vaulted wall-walks on the backs of such defences. Another was the use of vaulted galleries on the battlements of both towers and walls to permit plunging fire through continuous machicolations (Michaudel 2006, pp. 117–19). Meanwhile the design of towers remained

LEFT
The gallery between the Roman theatre of Busra (left) and the main wall of the 13th-century fortress (right) is illuminated by light-wells from the main fighting platform above. (Author's photograph)

RIGHT
The best-preserved water-storage cistern in Saladin's castle of Sudr (Qal'at al-Gindi) had a mosque built over its vaulted roof, and was filled with water brought from a nearby *wadi*. (Author's photograph)

largely unchanged, with rectangular plans being preferred except where the lie of the land virtually imposed a rounded outline, as in parts of Cairo's citadel and the repaired ex-crusader castle of Marqab. The Ayyubid concept of 'great towers' was taken further with some massive structures being built around a central pillar, with shooting rooms off the central chambers.

While the fortifications of several coastal cities were strengthened, the Mamluk period also saw the construction of quite isolated coastal forts. This was more characteristic of Egypt than Syria–Palestine where most of the coastline was defended by relatively few major fortifications with quite small garrisons but numerous observation points. For example, the port of Tripoli (now the suburb of al-Mina) initially had only two separated towers, though eventually six or even seven such towers overlooked the old harbour and a length of coast to the east. The spaces between them were defined by the ranges of the defensive siege engines at the time they were built. Thus the first to fourth towers are only 300m apart whereas the fifth and sixth are 1,000m and 1,200m from each other and the rest – the former being the effective range

LEFT
The aqueduct that brought water from the Nile to the Citadel of Cairo was first built during the reign of Sultan al-Nasir around 1311. From the mosque and *sabil* public fountain of Azdamur (centre) to the Citadel, it ran along the fortified city wall built during the reign of Saladin. (Author's photograph)

RIGHT
A 'shooting gallery' inside the upper part of the early 13th-century southern wall of the Citadel of Damascus. (Author's photograph)

26

of stone-throwing mangonels, whereas the latter was the effective range of early cannon (Sauvaget 1938,pp. 1–25).

Amongst the more isolated inland military buildings of the Mamluk sultanate, those associated with the *barid* government postal service were separate from the caravansarai system and were not designed to accommodate caravans. In their early form these buildings were divided into three parts consisting of a central courtyard, with living quarters for the men, plus a small *musallah* or prayer room, ablutions and latrine on one side, and stables for animals on the other (Sauvaget 1941).

The high status that architects enjoyed throughout Islamic history was certainly true of the Mamluk sultanate. Sultan al-Zahir Barquq who ruled twice (1382–89 and 1390–99), gave his daughter in marriage to his senior engineer al-Muhandis ('the engineer') Shihab al-Din Ahmad al-Tuluni. Within the Mamluk state heirarchy the office of *Muhandis al-'Ama'ir* ('Architect of Buildings') included responsibility for all major construction work, town planning, plus a major role in the selection of senior men employed in the building trade.

The Mongols and after

The devastation wrought by the invading Mongols across so much of the eastern Islamic world brought the development of military architecture to a virtual stop for several decades. Once most of the Mongol successor states had adopted Islam, however, there was a revival, and even some degree of innovation, though traditional building materials continued to be used. This usually meant mud-brick and fired-brick, but the citadel of Ardabil in north-western Iran was different, having a stone foundation of large masonry blocks above which the core of the wall itself and its bastions were of dark red, exceptionally hard, fired-brick. The main outer surfaces were then covered with much softer mud-bricks, which may have provided an effective cushion against mangonel stones (Pope 1939, p. 1245). Meanwhile in northern Iraq the fortified city of Mosul still formed a semi-circle on the west bank of the River Tigris. According to the Persian chronicler Hamidullah Mustawfi al-Qazwini, writing in the first half of the 14th century, it was still surrounded by a deep ditch, strong towers and high walls which ran down to the river and along its bank.

Some decades later the Spanish ambassador Clavijo provided a dramatic description of the citadel of Firuzkuh, which had recently fallen to Timur-i Lang:

> At the foot of the castle in the plain it is encircled by a wall defended by towers, and within this wall is the township; above this lower town wall is another higher up the slope, and again a third wall higher up still which is defended by its towers. Between these two last walls there were houses for the townsfolk, and above rose the bastions of the central fort with curtains very strongly built and flanked with many towers... Further in the fortress is found a copious spring of water gushing forth, sufficient to supply all its people.

The best-preserved medieval and post-medieval city walls in Iran are those of Yazd, which were built in 1119, rebuilt in 1137, and restored in the 14th century. In 1346 a new line of walls enclosed new suburbs, with many towers and seven gates covered in iron plates. Fifty years later a local ruler added a fosse. Nevertheless, the most impressive feature of Yazd's fortifications is the extended machicolations, which are relatively low down the wall, project outwards on brick corbels and have closely spaced apertures. The defences were further strengthened by a passage inside the city wall, essentially consisting of vaults connected by arches.

Elsewhere some unlikely buildings seem to have been either fortified or given symbolic fortifications, one such being the massive mausoleum of the Il-Khanid ruler Uljaitu Khudabanda Shah at Sultaniya. Here the surrounding wall was crowned with machicolations that were genuine enough for the complex to be described as a fortress.

Timur-i Lang's campaigns were as devastating as those of the Mongols, but he and his Timurid successors also built numerous, somewhat traditional fortifications. At the long-established military centre of Marw on the frontiers of Iran and Central Asia, for example, a new but considerably smaller fortress was built in 1409 by Timur-i Lang's son Shah Rukh. The walls of this Abdullah Khan Qal'a were mostly of mud-brick on a base of *pakhsa* blocks of rammed earth. Two styles have been found, the first being pierced with a single row of irregularly spaced arrow-slits, which are virtually identical to those in the neighbouring Seljuk fortified enclosure of Sultan Qal'a. The second type had a double row of slits, the upper perhaps for sighting and ventilation while the lower were probably for archery. The upper and lower slits were also staggered to avoid weakening the wall. At the end of the 15th century or a few decades later most of these fortifications were modified for cannon, the main wall and a *fausse-braie* ahead of it being raised, widened and strengthened with timber.

Timur-i Lang began building more isolated forts and fortresses in Central Asia early in his reign, one of the most interesting being Shahrukhia. This formidable fortress stood on the bank of the Syr Darya River and incorporated much of what remained of an older walled *shahristan* inner city and part of its similarly walled *rabad* outer suburb. Timur-i Lang's new wall had protruding semi-circular towers, two stories high, while the main entrance was protected by towers, which still survive.

Islamic India
Pre-Islamic India was particularly well fortified, with many different regional traditions developing, usually as a result of the availability of different

building materials and climatic conditions. The idea that the Indian subcontinent was invariably rich in good building stone is, for example, wrong. Some areas like Sind in what is now southern Pakistan were notably poor in this respect, as was much of the Punjab, and Bengal, where brick was the most common building material. Mountainous and densely forested Kashmir had plenty of stone, but evolved a highly sophisticated tradition of timber architecture, which contributed to some aspects of fortification.

The Meybod castle at Narin stands on the ancient caravan road between Isfahan and Yazd. Most of it probably dates from the 14th or 15th century. (ICHHTO)

In certain areas with suitable stone there was a tradition of fortification in which a rubble core was flanked by good quality ashlar masonry. Generally these walls were also strongly battered, meaning their outer and sometimes inner faces had a pronounced slope. It should nevertheless be borne in mind that in some respects mud-brick walls were better than those of stone and were clearly not an inferior or second-best choice. They could be easily razed if an area was about to be lost to the enemy, but were also quick and cheap to erect or re-erect if the fortunes of war changed. Of course, given the very seasonal nature of rainfall in much of India, the provision and security of adequate water supplies remained central to the design of Indian fortifications.

During the first stages of the Islamic conquest of much of northern India, the Muslims simply took over existing fortifications, but by the early 11th century clear differences had emerged between Islamic and Hindu military architecture. The fact that many of the known Muslim military engineers and architects in India had Turkish names could perhaps be linked with the emergence of these differing styles. One of the first examples of distinctive Indo-Islamic fortification was at Lal Kot, soon after the seven-gated Hindu fort at what became Delhi was conquered by the Muslims at the start of the 13th century.

The taking over and further development of pre-Islamic fortifications continued from the 14th to the 17th centuries as Muslim armies pushed further south into the Deccan area. For example, at Bijapur the Muslims made use of various pieces of early architecture, including temple columns and other fragments, in the guardroom of a fort which they strengthened in the 14th and 15th centuries. Not far away at Gulbarga, a fortress that was reused by its Muslim conquerors already had a doubled wall. Although there were only towers in the inner wall, these were strongly built, semi-circular structures to which barbettes were later added for gunpowder artillery. The Muslims also inherited the existing Hindu concept of the palace-fortress, which would be developed to an even more elaborate degree by India's Mughul emperors from the 16th to the 19th centuries.

Outside the Deccan region, though not in the more mountainous part of central India, the Muslim conquerors often made a point of straightening the walls of existing fortifications as part of their process of strengthening and modernization. In many cases, embrasures for light cannon were added

quite high up such walls at the end of the medieval period. What rarely changed were the strongly sloping outer faces of towers and bastions, which nevertheless rarely projected far ahead of the curtain walls. They in turn continued to contain uninterrupted galleries that sometimes also had external shooting galleries on their outer faces.

From at least the 14th century onwards, distinctive and characteristically Indian *chatris* kiosks were constructed on the summits of some citadel walls. These provided well-aired and relatively cool positions from which members of the ruling elite could see and, if necessary, be seen by their subjects. Gates were usually protected by flanking bastions, and in Dalautabad, according to one rather improbable story, a fixed brazier was used to fill a tunnel with smoke so that the enemy could not get through. A similarly bizarre, though not entirely impossible, version of this tale suggests that the brazier was used to make the upper iron door grating too hot for an enemy to handle and thus force open. Later medieval Indian fortifications may also have employed what could be seen as a local variation of the Central Asian and Afghan idea of using isolated, free-standing minarets as long-distance observation posts. At the same time some large, free-standing water towers apparently had the same secondary function.

THE LIVING SITES

Egypt and Syria before the Seljuks

The Middle East had a long tradition of public display by rulers and their courts. This was certainly true of the Fatimid caliphate where the fortified palace-city of al-Qahira (Cairo) became an arena for impressive displays of military power and religious authority. Sometimes it seemed as if such 'theatre' was to disguise the declining military might of the Fatimid caliphs and their senior *wazirs*, despite the fact that from the time of Badr al-Jamali in the late 11th century such *wazirs* effectively ruled the state as military dictators.

The most impressive military parades were when the caliph himself emerged from splendid seclusion in al-Qahira to take part in some important function. Clear attempts were made to ensure that the entrance to the ruler's fortified palace-city was similarly impressive and even intimidating. In fact, in many such palaces and citadels only the ruler was permitted to enter certain gates on horseback. Within several of these large fortified enclosures menageries of wild and exotic animals were used to further impress visitors, while the tradition of painting hunting and warlike scenes on certain walls still survived.

However, the smaller citadels of minor rulers could be far from impressive. Some might better be described as homely, such as the citadel of Shayzar, which was under Banu Munqidh rule until the earthquake of 1157. Usama Ibn Munqidh provides several fascinating bits of information in his memoirs, indicating, for example, that the household of the Banu Munqidh including the family members and their closest retainers or adherents had individual residences. They could incorporate towers, winding staircases and large windows with dramatic views. Yet these homes were almost certainly of the mixed mud-brick and stone construction that was traditional in this part of Syria, with rooms grouped around a courtyard, relating to which Usama mentioned arched porticos providing shade. Some were within the citadel while others, presumably of less senior families, were within the walled town.

The areas outside major fortified gates often had specific commercial, industrial or military functions. Writing in the late 14th and early 15th centuries, the historian al-Maqrizi noted that the Harat al-Husayniyya quarter, north of what was the Fatimid fortified palace-city of al-Qahira, was in two parts. That outside the Bab al-Futuh was where 'the soldiers' lived, the men in question presumably being members of the professional regiments, but not of the elite guard units who lived within the walled city. The second part of the Harat al-Husayniyya quarter lay outside the Bab al-Nasr and here a cemetery soon developed, initially for senior members of the ruling class, but later for the ordinary people of Cairo.

Life in and around less prestigious fortifications was more mundane, though during the mid-11th century the castle of Rahba was used as a storage depot for military equipment and a secure treasury for a local ruler. The leader on this occasion was al-Basasiri, a local Arab tribal chief whose death at the hands of the invading Seljuk Turks in 1059 marked the end of Arab political domination in Syria until after World War I. It is also worth noting that Qal'at Rahba again served as a major munitions depot on the Mamluk sultanate's tense Euphrates frontier.

The southern end of the citadel of Shayzar was separated from the rest of the hill by a deep, man-made fosse. (Author's photograph)

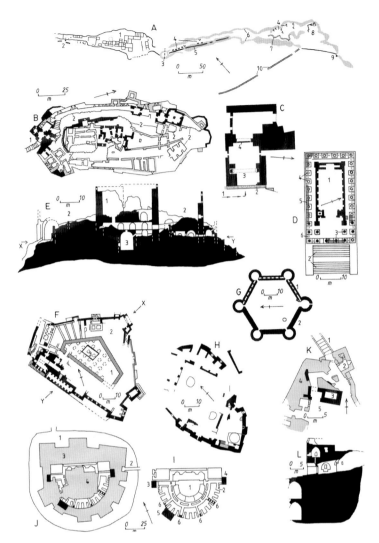

During this pre-Seljuk period, many castles owed their importance and wealth to their location on an important trade route. Shayzar, for example, controlled an important bridge over the River Orontes. Being one of the few safe crossing points it was jealously guarded, the Banu Munqidh building a small fort next to the bridge itself. This had to be almost continually manned during the 12th century because crusader-occupied territory lay only a few kilometres away.

Seljuks and Atabegs

Life in the fortified cities of the eastern Islamic world did not change during he 11th century. Inside its defences, Nishapur was already divided into 42 wards or quarters, the walled city and its suburbs now being one *farsakh* (6km) long and another broad. It had four gates through the fortifications of the old city proper, while another wall surrounded the suburb, all being dominated by the citadel with its two gates. Nishapur's main commercial roads ran across the city in straight lines which intersected at right angles, while water was supplied by canals which ran close to the city walls and also operated 70 mills.

Castles and small citadels.

A   Alamut, plan of early 13th-century mountain-top fortress.
1 Upper or main castle; 2 Cisterns; 3 Tunnel through rocky ridge; 4 Caves; 5 Fortifications of 'Onion Castle'; 6 Cliffs shown in grey; 7 Stepped pathway; 8 Foundations of buildings; 9 Fortified wall and tower; 10 *Qanat* canal. (After Willey)

B   Masyaf castle from the 12th to 14th centuries; early fortifications black; later fortifications grey. 1 Entrance path; 2 Structures cut from rock indicated by waving lines. (After Willey)

C   Masyaf; entrance complex. 1 Access path 2 Continuous machicolation above entrance; 3 So-called 'Frankish arch'; 4 Grooves for portcullis. (After Vondra)

D   Jarash, early 12th-century fortifications in Temple of Artemis. 1 Inner sanctum of Roman temple; 2 Entrance steps to temple; 3 Standing Roman columns shown black; 4 Collapsed or missing Roman columns as circles; 5 Existing 12th-century fortifications dark grey; 6 Presumed 12th-century fortifications light grey. (After Fisher)

E   Qal'at Rahba; vertical section between X and Y (see F). 1 Inner citadel; 2 Outer castle; 3 Cistern. (After Paillet)

F   Qal'at Rahba; plan of castle. X–Y line of section (see E); 1 Inner citadel; 2 Outer castle; 3 Cistern. Construction from the 11th to early 12th centuries shown black; from late

12th century and early 13th century dark grey; from later 13th to 15th centuries light grey. (After Paillet)

G   'Castle of Jalal al-Din' near Jajarm, probably 14th or 15th century. 1 Upper part of the wall showing 'jars' set into wall-walk; 2 Solid lower walls, with well in the south-western corner of courtyard. (After Diez)

H   Shumaymis castle; 13th-century fortifications shown black; later additions and strengthening shown grey. (After Bylinski)

I   Busra citadel in 12th century. 1 Roman theatre; 2 Eastern entrance unblocked; 3 Western fortified tower of 1089; 4 Eastern fortified tower of 1089; 5 South-western fortified tower built shortly before Second Crusade; 6 Entrances to Roman theatre walled up or considerably narrowed. (After Yovitchitch)

J   Busra citadel in 13th century. Fortifications added before 1150 shown black; Ayyubid and later structures grey. 1 Moat; 2 Entrance bridge; 3 Early 13th-century Ayyubid fortress enclosing Roman theatre; 4 Ayyubid palace in centre of theatre. (After Yovitchitch)

K   Shayzar Citadel; plan of the entrance complex. Byzantine, early Islamic and Munqidhite structures from before 1157 earthquake shown black; Zangid, Ayyubid and later rebuilding shown grey. (After Tonghini)

L   Shayzar Citadel; vertical section of the entrance complex. (After Tonghini)

Previously it had been unusual for rulers or governors to live in urban citadels, or hold court there. Instead many built fortified court-complexes some distance from the existing urban centres, Fatimid al-Qahira (Cairo) being one example. Some originally Turkish dynasties also clung to the old traditions; the palace of the Ghaznawid Sultan Mas'ud III (1099–1115), outside Ghazna itself, was a somewhat superficially fortified palace rather than a genuine citadel. The most distinctive feature of these palace complexes was that their outer walls were not attached to those of the neighbouring city. This resulted in a clear physical and symbolic separation between ruler and ruled. Meanwhile, most court ceremony and the activities of government were hidden from ordinary people, so that when the ruler and his entourage did emerge for a particular event, their appearance 'before the multitude' was even more significant.

Nevertheless, court life and that of the military elites started to change with the Seljuk Turkish conquests of the 11th century. A new form of court-citadel emerged in the late 11th-century Middle East, in areas ruled by the Great Seljuk sultanate. This was also a period of major changes in the recruitment, structure and reward of armies. Large forces of professional infantry were gradually supplanted, though not entirely replaced, by smaller forces of better paid and more highly trained cavalry of *mamluk* so-called 'slave' origin, supplemented by non-elite freeborn cavalry, usually of nomadic origin.

One of the less obvious impacts of this shift resulted from the fact that the men, if not the animals, of the elite or professional military elements needed less room than their predecessors. Gone were entire quarters of a city inhabited by soldiers. Instead, the younger *mamluks*, or *ghulams* as they were also known, mostly lived in barracks in or near their ruler's palace-citadel. Once they rose to higher rank they often moved into higher status houses, which also served as barracks for their own younger *mamluk* soldiers.

Nevertheless, it does seem that, for some centuries, the new political and military elites felt insecure and so needed fortified centres for themselves, their families, adherents and wealth. The resulting court-citadels continued to separate ruling groups from the bulk of the population, but, being attached to the main city or even located within its walls, they permitted closer interaction between rulers and ruled. Of course, there were also more immediate military concerns behind such architectural developments. This was especially true in the Middle Eastern heartlands, which were, or were feared to be, under direct threat from the Crusades.

One of the earliest identifiable such court-citadels was in Damascus. Despite the fact that the centre of the city rose slightly higher than its surroundings, being a *tel* formed by millennia of human habitation, this was not dominant enough to attract the Seljuks as a site for a new citadel. It would also have been entirely surrounded by an Arabic-speaking and, at that date, largely Shi'a Muslim urban population. So the Turkish-speaking and Sunni Muslim Seljuk rulers of Damascus chose an already administrative, if not yet particularly military, site at the north-western corner of the city.

The Arab Mirdasid dynasty, which ruled much of northern Syria in the 11th century, had used the *tel* in Aleppo as an administrative centre, but it was Nur al-Din who ordered its major transformation. He built a palace known as the Dar al-Dhahab or 'House of Gold', renovated two *maqams* or shrines, one of which was associated with the Old Testament Prophet Abraham, and rebuilt the minimal fortifications, which seem to have fallen into decay. The citadel now became a true courtly centre with palatial, military and administrative buildings, plus a *hamam* bath.

Iran and its neighbours

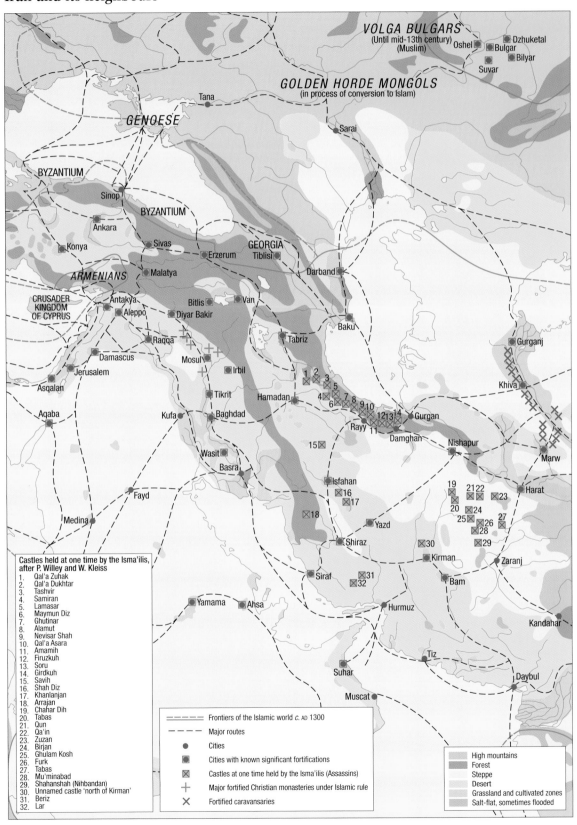

VOLGA BULGARS
(Until mid-13th century)
(Muslim)

Oshel • Dzhuketal
Bulgar
Bilyar
Suvar

GOLDEN HORDE MONGOLS
(in process of conversion to Islam)

Tana
Sarai

GENOESE

BYZANTIUM

Sinop

BYZANTIUM

Ankara

Konya

Sivas

Erzerum

GEORGIA
Tiblisi

Darband

ARMENIANS

Malatya

Antakya

Bitlis • Van

Baku

CRUSADER
KINGDOM
OF CYPRUS

Aleppo

Diyar Bakir

Gurganj

Raqqa

Mosul

Tabriz

Khiva

Damascus

Irbil

Jerusalem

Tikrit

Hamadan

Asqalan

Kufa

Baghdad

Gurgan

Aqaba

Rayy

Damghan

Nishapur

Wasit

Marw

Fayd

Basra

Isfahan

Harat

Medina

Yazd

Kirman

Shiraz

Zaranj

Yamama • Ahsa

Siraf

Hurmuz

Bam

Kandahar

Suhar

Tiz

Muscat

Daybul

Castles held at one time by the Isma'ilis, after P. Willey and W. Kleiss
1. Qal'a Zuhak
2. Qal'a Dukhtar
3. Tashvir
4. Samiran
5. Lamasar
6. Maymun Diz
7. Ghutinar
8. Alamut
9. Nevisar Shah
10. Qal'a Asara
11. Amamih
12. Firuzkuh
13. Soru
14. Girdkuh
15. Savih
16. Shah Diz
17. Khanlanjan
18. Arrajan
19. Chahar Dih
20. Tabas
21. Qun
22. Qa'in
23. Zuzan
24. Birjan
25. Ghulam Kosh
26. Furk
27. Tabas
28. Mu'minabad
29. Shahanshah (Nihbandan)
30. Unnamed castle 'north of Kirman'
31. Beriz
32. Lar

----- Frontiers of the Islamic world *c.* AD 1300
- - - Major routes
● Cities
▣ Cities with known significant fortifications
⊠ Castles at one time held by the Isma'ilis (Assassins)
✛ Major fortified Christian monasteries under Islamic rule
✕ Fortified caravansaries

High mountains
Forest
Steppe
Desert
Grassland and cultivated zones
Salt-flat, sometimes flooded

Nur al-Din's brothers and successors of the Zangid dynasty, as well as the rival Artuqid Turkish dynasty in south-eastern Anatolia, adopted the same policy. They and their immediate retinue now lived within urban citadels while the majority of the mostly Turkish tribesmen who formed their main power base lived outside the city. Elsewhere in the Jazira region the tumultuous late 11th and early 12th centuries led to the virtual abandonment of some fortified towns and the neglect of their defences. In normal times one of the main functions of such places had been to defend local trade routes and communications. Despite the prevailing chaos in some areas, this duty still fell on the shoulders of local governors. Protection also came from the local *shihna*, consisting of lower status professional troops maintained by the nearest 'officer in charge of urban garrisons'. Reference to one such *shihna* in early 12th-century northern Syria stated that it only numbered 10 horsemen.

Another feature of fortified cities and their citadels, which would become more important as the decades passed, were *maydans*. These open spaces were used for military training as well as parades and various non-military purposes. One of the main open spaces in 11th-century Nishapur was known as the Maydan al-Husayniyyin, but there is no evidence that it was mainly used for military purposes. The *maydan* of early 12th-century Mardin was directly beneath the walls of the citadel, whereas a generation or so later Nur

ABOVE LEFT
The walled city of Hisn Kayfa (Hasankayf) overlooking the River Tigris was the capital of a militarily significant state ruled by a branch of the Turkish Artuqid dynasty. (Author's photograph)

ABOVE RIGHT
The caravansarai of Khan al-Arus was built by Saladin in the late 12th century, but was then restored several times. (Author's photograph)

BELOW
The exterior of the Agzikarakhan highlights the fortified character of these early 13th-century Turkish 'medieval motels'. Though the decoration is confined to the entrance it is nevertheless quite elaborate. (Author's photograph)

The Burj al-Gharbi 'Western Tower' is virtually all that remains of the medieval urban fortifications of Alexandria, and was built upon the foundations of the previous Roman defences. (Author's photograph)

al-Din had the Maydan al-Akhdar, the 'green' or 'grassy' *maydan*, laid out on top of the *tel* of Aleppo when he built the city's first real citadel.

At Mosul the *maydan* was specifically stated to be within the city wall during the later 12th and early 13th century, but was nevertheless still separated from the main city by another fortified wall. It was also said to be near the 11th-century Uqaylid and 12th-century Zangid city walls, and was where troops quartered; whether this meant permanent barracks or temporary encampments in time of crisis is unclear. The Zangid local ruler 'Izz al-Din Ma'sud had a 'kiosk' erected in or next to this *maydan*. 'Imad al-Din Zangi, the founder of the Zangid dynasty, allowed one of his senior *amirs* to build a house 'a mangonel throw's distance' from the citadel, and less than a century later this building had become the *madrasa* of the mother of al-Malik al-Salih. The same area also became known as the *Dur al-Mamluka* (government offices), while a neighbouring market area specifically served the needs of the nearby *maydan* called the *Mahalla Suq al-Turkman* (dismounting or unloading place of the market of the Turcomans).

At the time of the siege of Damascus by the Second Crusade, that city already had two *maydans*. These were the 'green' or 'grassy' *maydan* next to the River Barada which was used for military and other purposes. The second was the 'stoney' *maydan*, a larger area south-west of the city of Damascus, which may have been more of a mustering point; it was also used for various types of market.

Within the main fortified towns and cities of the newly created Turkish states in what is now Turkey, there tended to be clear differences between the opulence of the citadel and centre, the prosperity of the main town within its walls, and the sometimes acute poverty, indeed squalor, of the suburbs. The towns themselves were organized along what were now well-established medieval Islamic lines, based upon the urban structures that had developed during the early medieval golden age of the 'Abbasid caliphate. This resulted in a clear separation between different craft quarters. In many places quarters were also distinguished by the ethnic origins and religious affiliations of the majority of their inhabitants.

Tensions between such groups, and the need to strengthen the city's defences, resulted in such quarters occasionally being separated by further fortified walls. By the early 13th century, when the Seljuk Sultanate of Rum reached a peak of prosperity, towns like Konya, Kayseri and Sivas had populations of over 100,000. Indeed, Konya, as the capital of this flourishing Seljuk state, had changed from a nomadic encampment around a decayed Romano-Byzantine town in the 12th century, to a luxurious city by the 14th century.

The Ayyubids

The development of the court-citadel continued under the Ayyubid dynasty. The most obvious was, of course, in the main Ayyubid capital city of Cairo, where the citadel started by Saladin was eventually completed by his Ayyubid and Mamluk successors. It eventually housed a royal residence which itself included a great *iwan* throne or reception hall, various smaller residences, mosques, stables, barracks, a royal library and the *wazir* or chief minister's residence. Around the outside of the fortifications of this citadel, though at a lower level, a number of large civic and charitable building projects seem to have served as a sort of buffer zone between the citadel, as seat of government, and the general populace of Cairo. The only change was during latter part of the first half of the 13th century, when Sultan al-Malik al-Salih built a new fortified court-citadel on the island of Rawda (Roda) in the Nile, connected to the older south-western part of the city of Cairo by a major new bridge.

A tower and some sections of the late-medieval city fortifications of Yazd in south-central Iran. Although they are made of mud-brick, they survive remarkably intact because this central desert region is one of the driest in Iran. (ICHHTO)

Damascus was the second city of the Ayyubid 'family sultanate', but the decoration of the citadel, as massively rebuilt by al-'Adil, was conservative when compared to similarly dated buildings in northern Syria, especially in Aleppo. Perhaps this rather plain style was considered more suited to what became a substantial, Damascus-based, military construction industry, which carried out fortification projects in many places, not least those regained from the Crusader States. We know a great deal about how court ceremony was organized within the citadel of Damascus. For example, the ruler always sat in the northern *iwan* or arched recess of the assembly or reception hall – perhaps because here he faced the *qibla* or direction of Mecca.

More personal details of everyday life in an Ayyubid fortress can be seen in the ruined castle of Subayba. Here one of most interesting architectural features was a water elevation system close to, but separate from, a lower latrine located nearby, so that it could be easily flushed or cleaned. Water was pulled up a shaft, the upper entrance of which was inside a blind arch near the castle gate. Another human detail was a gaming board consisting of three concentric rectangles crudely carved into one of the steps of the

The eastern provinces

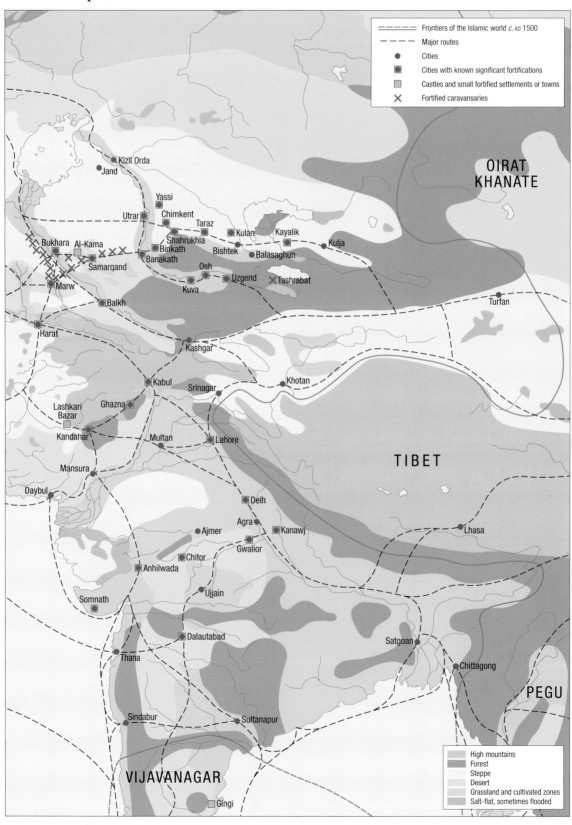

Frontiers of the Islamic world c. AD 1500
Major routes
Cities
Cities with known significant fortifications
Castles and small fortified settlements or towns
Fortified caravansaries

OIRAT KHANATE

Kizil Orda
Jand
Yassi
Chimkent
Utrar
Taraz
Kulan
Kayalik
Kulja
Bukhara
Al-Kama
Shahrukhia
Binkath
Bishtek
Balasaghun
Banakath
Samarqand
Osh
Uzgend
Kuva
Tashrabat
Marw
Balkh
Turfan
Harat
Kashgar
Kabul
Srinagar
Khotan
Ghazna
Lashkari Bazar
Kandahar
Multan
Lahore
TIBET
Mansura
Daybul
Delh
Agra
Ajmer
Kanawj
Lhasa
Gwalior
Chitor
Anhilwada
Ujjain
Somnath
Dalautabad
Satgoan
Thana
Chittagong
PEGU
Sindabur
Sultanapur
VIJAVANAGAR
Gingi

High mountains
Forest
Steppe
Desert
Grassland and cultivated zones
Salt-flat, sometimes flooded

entrance complex inside the defences. Perhaps it was made by bored sentries, another being found on the threshold of the castle's east door (Hartal 2001).

Mamluks, Mongols and Timurids

Life for the civilian population within the fortified places of the Mamluk sultanate initially went on much as it had done under the Ayyubids. The crusader threat had dwindled, whereas there had been significant shifts in population as a result of Mongol invasions. In Rahba large numbers of refugees arrived from territory now ruled by the Mongol Il-Khans. The lower, riverside town of Mayadin was virtually abandoned as its inhabitants either moved to a newer town close to the citadel or fled westwards.

The fortress of Bitlis is a mixture of early Islamic, Armenian, Kurdish and Turkish construction techniques, though the use of variously shaped towers was an Armenian tradition. (Author's photograph)

Even in cities and towns less exposed than Rahba or Aleppo, the Mamluk state developed an urban nightwatch, which was in effect a police force, responsible for maintaining order and stopping burglars. However, the street lighting, which amazed many European visitors, was not a new concept. A virtual curfew was announced each nightfall by drums or bells, while a bell was also used in some fortified places to announce the changing of the guard (Ziadeh 1953, pp. 109–11). Another feature that impressed most western visitors was the Mamluk pigeon-post, a highly sophisticated government communications system maintained and operated by paid officials. Most cities seemingly had at least one pigeon-loft for this purpose.

Major fortresses of course had their own arsenals or stores of arms and armour, some apparently serving as regional depots for military equipment or for the grain that would be needed by field armies. The remains of two arsenals or workshops have been found in the citadel of Damascus; one dates from the late 13th and 14th centuries, the other from the closing decades of Mamluk rule in the late 15th and early 16th centuries. On the other hand, even the most important arsenals sometimes ran short, as described by Ibn Sasra in his *Chronicle of Damascus* when, at a military review in 1392, several of the *halqa* or non-*mamluk* troops in Damascus had to share the same hat and sword, swapping before going into the presence of the governor of the city.

Other sources make it clear that citadels played a part in more popular forms of ceremony or entertainment. In the early 15th century, for example, the Burgundian traveller Bertrandon de la Brocquière saw various festivities in Damascus, one of which included the firing of cannon – presumably with blank shot – from the citadel while the inhabitants of the city joined in with small 'hand-cannons' or fireworks attached to wooden poles.

Details about life within the remaining fortifications of the eastern Islamic world in the aftermath of the Mongol invasions are sparse. In fact, it is really only after the Islamification of the Mongol conquerors and under their successors that such information re-emerges. By then little seems to have changed, and citadels, for example, continued to serve their traditional functions as centres of settled and urban authority in the face of all too often threatening tribal and nomadic power. The citadel of Harat, for example, housed the court of the 14th-century Kart dynasty in what are now the borderlands of Iran and Afghanistan, and included a treasury, prison, place of execution as well as reception halls. Many of these later medieval, eastern Islamic fortified cities still served as protected centres of trade.

Despite the devastation and slaughter that Timur-i Lang inflicted on much of the eastern Islamic world, he and his successors encouraged trade and urban life once a region was under their control. Samarqand was the capital of Timur's ephemeral empire, and its citadel was described in detail by the visiting Spanish ambassador Clavijo:

> At one end of the city there is a castle, which is defended on one side by a stream flowing through a deep ravine and is very strong. The lord [Timur] kept his treasure in that castle and none may enter it except the magistrate and his officers. In this castle the lord has as many as a thousand captives [mostly from Damascus], who were skilled workmen, and laboured all the year around at making scale cuirasses and light helmets, and bows and arrows.

The so-called Castle of Jalal al-Din was located in the fertile agricultural area around Jajarm, close to a gap between rows of hills, where it was probably intended to inhibit Turcoman raiders from the north attacking a caravan route that ran through Jajarm. Having been of relatively minor significance in the early medieval period, this had now become the main east–west trading link in this part of Iran.

During the last centuries of the Middle Ages, the steadily expanding Islamic states of the Indian subcontinent developed their own highly distinctive forms of social organization within their many strongly fortified cities and citadels. Here it is clear that some architectural features continued to be used for decorative reasons long after their original military purpose was outdated. They appear, for example, on many non-military structures such as the seemingly fortified tombs of Muslim rulers and other high-ranking personages outside some cities. Having sometimes been interpreted as 'fortified outworks', they are now mostly seen for what they really were – buildings that were given decorative fortified features for cultural and religious reasons.

The major fortresses of Islamic India remained real enough, however, awe-inspiring court-citadels being particularly important in areas where the bulk of the urban population remained Hindu. Most of the 'seven cities' that made up the history of Delhi were court-citadels, though frequent rebuilding and subsequent changes in the layouts often makes it difficult to interpret their original plans.

THE SITES AT WAR

The Middle East before the Seljuks

Strangely enough there is less detailed information about later medieval Islamic fortifications in time of war then there is about these sites in times of peace, particularly where isolated castles and urban defences are concerned. However, we know that the citadel of al-Hadba overlooking Mosul in northern Iraq had a garrison of 1,500 soldiers in 1108–09, while in 1071 the fortifications of Aleppo had been strong enough to resist the Seljuk Turks. Despite a bombardment which probably used larger stone-throwing weapons than are usually thought to exist at that time, the Turks were unable to destroy or capture the tower that they were focussing upon, though in the end a blockade convinced the citizens of Aleppo to negotiate a Seljuk takeover.

A generation later the fanatical hordes of the First Crusade besieged the small fortified town of al-Bara. Here the defenders fought hand-to-hand with spears against those manning the wooden siege tower that the crusaders

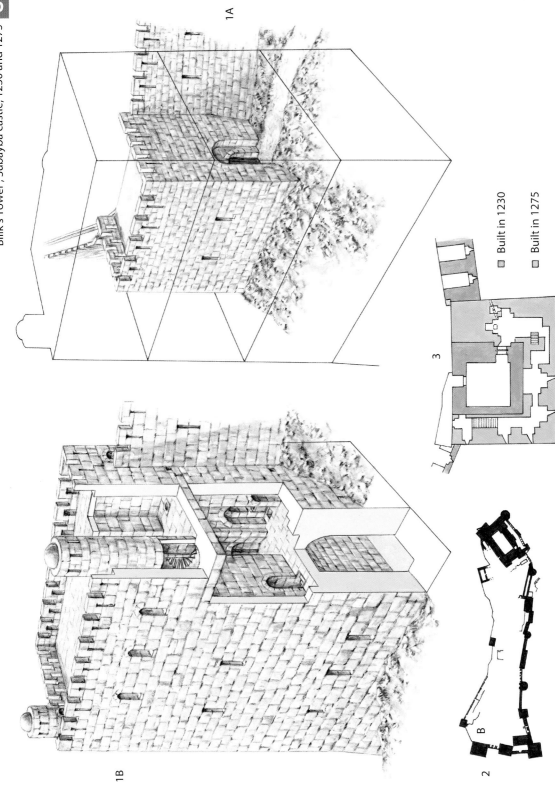

'Bilik's Tower', Subayba castle, 1230 and 1275

1A

1B

3

2

B

☐ Built in 1230

☐ Built in 1275

The multiple outer walls of the now abandoned fortified medieval city of Samarqand were largely of *pakhsa* or large mud-bricks. (Author's photograph)

The castle of Qa'in was one of the most important Isma'ili fortresses in the Kuhistan eastern region of Iran. (Peter Willey)

rolled against their wall. The technological capabilities of the garrisons and inhabitants of the Syrian coastal cities was greater; those attacked during and immediately after the First Crusade used elaborate defensive machines made of timber and operated by ropes. Such skills surely reflected the maritime heritage of these coastal peoples, while their skill with advanced incendiary weapons probably stemmed from the same source.

During the early 12th century, Islamic forces in the Middle East used large stone-throwing siege artillery more in defence than attack. Yet the idea that

D   'BILIK'S TOWER', SUBAYBA CASTLE, 1230 AND 1275

The construction of much larger towers was the most obvious development in 13th-century Islamic military architecture. An interesting example was built by the Mamluk *amir* Badr al-Din Bilik al-Khaznadar at the north-western edge of the Subayba castle on the Golan Heights. The original castle, built between 1228 and 1230, was badly damaged during the Mongol invasion of Syria, though the north-western tower survived reasonably intact. In 1275 the *amir* Bilik had three massive new towers constructed, entirely enclosing the earlier ones, including the north-western tower shown

here (after Hartal 2001). Beyond it is an unaltered early 13th-century tower in the north wall while to the right is the more substantial western curtain wall.

1A The early 13th-century north-western tower, with the outline of 'Bilik's Tower' shown around it.
1B 'Bilik's Tower', which enclosed the early 13th-century tower.
2   Plan of Subayba castle (after Deschamps 1939).
    A Keep and governor's palace; B Later 13th-century 'Bilik's Tower' enclosing an early 13th-century tower.
3   Plan of the first-floor level of 'Bilik's Tower' (after Hartal 2001).

A communications and fighting gallery inside the curtain wall of the Citadel of Cairo, just south of Burj al-Ramlah tower, built or started during the reign of Saladin. (Author's photograph)

restricted use reflected a shortage of skilled carpenters compared to an abundance of such skills amongst crusaders from a forested Europe stretches the argument too far. The Muslim military heritage of cautious warfare with a minimum expenditure of treasure and blood probably lay behind a preference for prolonged sieges and blockades rather than direct assaults.

The Great Seljuks

Siege warfare barely changed under the Great Seljuk sultans and their successors, this minimal Central Asian or Iranian influence reflecting the fact that, by the time the Seljuks extended their control across most of the eastern and central Muslim regions, the Islamic world had already firmly established military traditions to which the Turks could add little.

Siege warfare in the smaller Middle Eastern states that escaped Great Seljuk domination or emerged as *atabeg* principalities varied. In many places pre-Seljuk traditions, ideas or technologies reappeared, while evidence from crusader sources confirms the characteristic caution of their foes. Usama Ibn Munqidh describes how on one occasion the Franks tried to take Shayzar by trickery, probably in 1122:

One day we rose early in the morning at the time of the dawn prayer only to find a band of Franks, about ten horsemen, who had come to the gate of the lower town before it was opened. They asked the gatekeeper, 'What is the name of this town?' The gate was of wood with beams running across, and the gatekeeper was inside of the gate. 'Shayzar', he replied. The Franks thereupon shot an arrow at him, through the crack of the door, and they turned back with their horses trotting under them… I said to my uncle, 'Command only, and

OPPOSITE PAGE: Late medieval fortifications

A   Alexandria in the 14th century. **1** Western harbour; **2** Eastern harbour; **3** Ruins of ancient lighthouse; **4** Tower of Sultan al-Nasir; **5** Canal from Nile; **6** Doubled wall facing western harbour; **7** Bab al-Akhdar 'Green Gate'; **8** Bab al-Bahr 'Sea Gate'; **9** Bab al-Rashid 'Rosetta Gate'; **10** Bab al-Sidrah 'Gate of the Pillars'; **11** Ribat al-Siwar and Ribat al-Wasiti; **12** Arsenal; **13** Governor's palace; **14** Weapons depot and Sultan's palace; **15** 'Mosque of Alexander the Great' and Mosque of al-Mu'tamin; **16** Islamic tombs. (After Christie)

B   Shahrukhia in 15th century showing surviving walls and towers. **1** *Shahristan* fortified town; **2** So-called Timur's settlement, perhaps citadel; **3** Moat. (After Buryakov)

C   Marw, Abdullah Khan Qal'a, reconstructions of early 15th-century fortifications. **1** Elevation; **2** Depth of moat; **3** Plan; **4** Section through wall and side view of tower. (After Buryakov)

D   Tripoli, late 14th-century 'Lions Tower', vertical section. **1** First floor; **2** Ground floor; **3** Entrance; **4** Cistern. (After Sauvaget)

E   Tripoli, the 'Lions Tower', plan of ground floor. **1** Entrance; **2** Opening into cistern; **3** Stairs to upper floors. (After Sauvaget)

F   Tripoli, the 'Lions Tower', plan of first floor. **1** Entrance from ground floor; **2** Stairs to roof. (After Sauvaget)

G   Tripoli, painted Mamluk heraldic insignia in 'Lions Tower'. (After Sauvaget)

H   Rashid, illustration of late 15th-century fort of Qayit Bay in 1737. (From F. L. Norden, *Voyage d'Égypte et de Nubie,* Paris, 1775)

I   Rashid, plan of fort of Qayit Bay. **1** Storage rooms; **2** Mosque; **3** Minaret; **4** Well; **5** Napoleonic bastions around original towers. (After De Cosson)

J   Qasr al-Tina, plan of 15th-century fort. (After Tamari)

K   Harat, plan of 15th-century fortified city. **1** Upper citadel; **2** Outer bailey of citadel; **3** Great mosque; **4** Roads and tracks; **5** Canals and seasonal riverbeds; **6** Cemetery. (After Allen, Bruno and Perbellini)

R SYR DARYA

A

B

C

D

E

F

G

H

R.NILE

I

J

K

45

I shall take our companions, pursue the enemy and dislodge them from their saddles as long as they are not so far away'. 'No', replied my uncle, who was more of an expert in warfare than I was. 'Is there a Frank in Syria who knows not Shayzar? This is a ruse.'

The entrance passage of the upper gate complex of the Citadel of Aleppo was protected by a series of box machicolations. However, their cramped interiors must have reduced their effectiveness, a man having to kneel to get inside. (Fred Nicolle and author's photograph)

He was right, as the army of Antioch was to be found waiting in ambush behind Tal-Milh ('Salty Hill'). Usama also describes a tale told to him by Khutlukh, one of his father's *mamluks*, of the full-scale Byzantine siege in 1137–38, when the enemy bombarded Shayzar with mangonels:

> We were once sitting in the hallway at the entrance of the castle with our full equipment and swords. All of a sudden an old man appeared running towards us and said, 'O Moslems! Your private family quarters! The Rumis have entered the town'. We immediately grasped our swords and went out to find that they had already climbed through a breach in the outer wall, which their mangonels had made [suggesting particularly powerful trebuchets]. So we applied our swords on them until we repulsed them, and we pursued them until we got them as far back as their comrades.

Shortly afterwards another mangonel stone killed the old man who had brought the warning, as he was relieving himself against a wall.

A citadel was supposed to be militarily self-sufficient, especially in its water supply, but in weaker citadels insecure sources of drinking water often made a separate resistance impossible. At Baalbak, for example, the garrison of the ancient temple complex relied upon water from the town, until a major

E   KARAMAN CASTLE, MID-14TH CENTURY

Karaman Castle was rebuilt several times. The earliest parts date from the 12th century when the Seljuk Sultanate of Rum constructed the citadel on top of a low hill as the strongest point of the city's urban fortifications. It was strengthened in 1356 by the Karamanoglu dynasty, when the castle consisted of short stretches of curtain wall with large, closely spaced towers.

The mixture of round, polygonal and rectangular towers shows the eclectic character of Anatolian Turkish military architecture, which drew upon Islamic, Byzantine, Armenian and even Western European ideas. In this reconstruction the level open area next to the citadel is being used as a *maydan* or training ground, as was common across almost all the Islamic world.

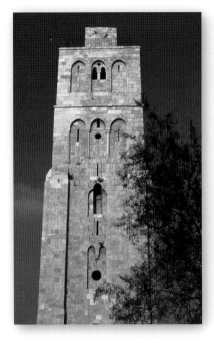

LEFT
The sturdily built minaret of the late 13th-century 'White Tower Mosque' at Ramlah is perhaps the most obviously military of such exceptionally large minarets. (Author's photograph)

RIGHT
Al-Minarah, 'The Minaret', is the only structure still standing amid the ruins of the medieval city of Wasit. It consists of the 14th-century, brick-built north gate flanked by the minarets of an attached mosque.
(Iraqi Ministry of Antiquities)

Seljuk stucco decoration in one of the most palatial buildings in the fortified strategic city of Marw, dating from between 1118 and 1157.

upgrading of the fortifications in the later 12th century. In practical terms, the function of most urban citadels was simply to strengthen one part – often the weakest – of a city's fortifications. The size of the city was another major consideration. When 'Imad al-Din Zangi attempted to besiege Amida (now Diyar Bakir) his army was unable to surround the walls, so they attempted to encourage its surrender by progressively cutting down the valuable surrounding orchards.

Baghdad, even in its shrunken 12th- and 13th-century form, posed an even greater problem; so much so that in the mid-1130s a night-time sortie by a large force defeated part of the Great Seljuk sultan Ma'sud's besieging army. However, Baghdad's size would not save it from the huge army that the Mongols could field, and actually may have made the city more difficult to defend in 1258. Ibn Tiqtaqa's account of the fall of the 'Abbasid caliphate included details he learned from the nephew of the caliph's *wazir*, who survived this catastrophe: 'The people unexpectedly saw the Mongol standards appear on the wall of Baghdad by the tower called the Persian Tower, near one of the gates of Baghdad called the Kalwadha Gate. This tower was the shortest of the wall' (Kritzeck and Winder 1959, p. 179).

Other great Islamic cities had by then already fallen to the Mongols, some after an epic siege, others after only token resistance. According to the 13th-century Persian chronicler 'Uthman Ibn Siraj al-Din al-Juzjani, during the conquest of Harat one of the defenders was a *ghazi* (religiously motivated volunteer) wearing full armour, helmet and weapons. He lost his footing on the rampart, fell and rolled down the glacis before being taken prisoner. The superstitious Mongols regarded the fact that he was unhurt as a miracle and so allowed the *ghazi* to live (Maulana Minhaj al-Din 1970, p. 1,039).

The Seljuk Sultanate of Rum in Anatolia was also invaded and forced into vassal status by the Mongols. Here, Kayseri was often selected as a suitable place for mustering and reviewing armies before a summer campaign. On such occasions there would be various forms of entertainment for the troops, including poets, jugglers, displays of horsemanship, associated military skills and, of course, feasting.

Ayyubids and Mamluks

A number of military manuals written during the late 12th- and 13th-century Ayyubid period show how the governors, garrisons and inhabitants of a fortified place were expected to behave before and during a siege. These were largely based upon earlier 'Abbasid military texts, but also seem to reflect current reality. In fact the similarities between such advice and sieges described in Ayyubid chronicles can be quite striking. One of the most practical manuals was written for Saladin and his immediate successors by Abu'l-Hassan 'Ali al-Harawi, whose Chapter 13 includes sections on the materials to be stored in arsenals. Chapter 23 looks at the defensive aspects of siege warfare, advising a ruler or governor to take council with masons, sappers, crossbowmen, javelin throwers, mangonel operators and other specialists. It places great emphasis on the need to poison wells and pollute water sources, which besiegers were expected to rely upon, as well as attempts to spread disease amongst the attackers, though this should only be done downwind of the defenders' own positions. The garrison were advised to attack the besiegers' encampment while it was being set up; this attack being carried out by cavalry with plenty of archers, *naft* incendiary material throwers and those armed with crossbows. Thereafter the garrison should continue to make as many sorties as possible during the darkest nights, again using incendiary weapons.

Coastal cities could face specific problems when attacked. During the Fifth Crusade's siege of Dimyat (Damietta), the defending garrison was able to retain control of an island tower that secured one end of a chain blocking navigation up the Nile for larger ships. The crusaders were unable to place scaling ladders against its walls until they had lashed two ships together and erected a fireproof wooden platform on four masts or spars. The shallow

The castle of Baltit before its recent restoration. The architectural style, making considerable use of timber as well as stone, is partly Central Asian and partly north-western Indian. (Peter Willey)

draught of the two ships in question enabled the men on this platform to get close enough to take control of the top of the tower.

A few decades earlier Saladin had besieged Amida (Diyar Bakir), where his siege engineers used stone-throwing mangonels to destroy the battlements and drive defending archers from the wall. The mangonels did not attempt to knock down the weaker outer wall but merely toppled its parapet and crenellations, thus permitting attackers to assault the outer fortifications with scaling ladders.

An even larger number of military manuals survive from the Mamluk period, though most of their authors merely assembled existing and sometimes outdated ideas. One of those who did include both new and traditional ideas was a retired Mamluk officer, Ibn Urunbugha al-Zardkash, whose enthusiastic interest in siege and naval technology reflected the growing importance of a variety of more developed and, indeed, entirely new weaponry in the 15th century. Al-Zardkash placed great emphasis on how to assemble mangonels and other siege weapons on top of towers and fortified walls.

By this date firearms were widespread in the Islamic Middle East. The early appearance and use of gunpowder has attracted a great deal of scholarly interest, though it should be pointed out that the weapons themselves did not become important in siege warfare until the later 14th century. By the start of the 16th century, however, it is clear that the Mamluk sultanate had many heavy cannon, though all seem to have been based in the main citadels, most notably Cairo, where they were intended for fixed defence.

Warfare along the Mamluk sultanate's threatened frontier in Syria largely revolved around the holding or regaining of fortified places. When the Mongol Il-Khans of Iran and Iraq were the main threat, Mamluk strategy was straightforward, being based upon the key frontier castles of al-Bira in the north-west and al-Rahba in the south-east, both of which were attacked on numerous occasions. During the reign of Sultan Baybars (1260–77) al-Bira was sometimes called 'the lock of Syria' and suffered more Mongol attacks than any other fortress. Yet it withstood most of them, largely because the Mamluk state's efficient communications and mustering system enabled relief forces to intervene in time.

Both these strongly garrisoned castles were connected to the centres of command in Damascus and Cairo by pigeon post, *barid* messengers and chains of beacon fires. Both also guarded important fords across the Euphrates River frontier and served as forward warning stations. Furthermore, they acted as intelligence-gathering centres and bases from where Mamluk forces could raid enemy territory.

While the desert and steppes formed a defensive barrier to the east and north-east, the far northern frontier of the Mamluk sultanate was more exposed to both Armenian and Mongol attack. However, the situation stabilized after Baybars regained several fortresses, included Baghras and Darbassak, and the city of Antioch in 1268, thus shortening the frontier between the Euphrates and the Mediterranean Sea.

Meanwhile the approaches to the main northern Syrian city of Aleppo were protected by small fortified towns like 'Ayn Tab and Azaz, which, like the Euphrates castle to the east, served as observation points facing north. On the other hand, some fortifications were not repaired after being destroyed by the Mongols and retaken by the Mamluks. They included Tal Bashir, Burj al-Rasas and Harim, though they were apparently garrisoned. Mamluk troops were spread dangerously thin in these areas and perhaps such garrisons were not considered strong enough to hold these castles, merely using them as bases.

The fortifications on Jazirat Fara'un were once thought to be the crusader castle of the Ile de Graye. In fact it was built on the orders of Saladin shortly before his great victory over the crusader Kingdom of Jerusalem at the battle of Hattin. (Author's photograph)

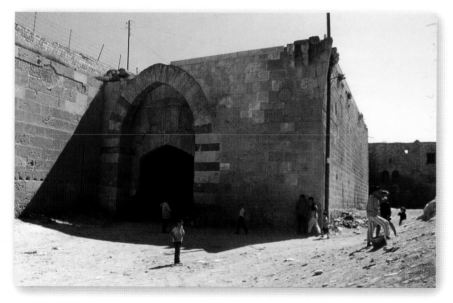

The Bab Kinnisrin or main southern gate of the fortified medieval city of Aleppo, photographed in the early 1970s before it was cleared, cleaned and restored. (Author's photograph)

LEFT
A carved monumental
inscription filling one course of
masonry on the outside of the
inner citadel of Salkhad, dating
from the Ayyubid period.
(Author's photograph)

RIGHT
After the Muslims captured
the crusader castle of Saone
(Sahyun) they added a palace,
a *hamam* bathhouse, a mosque
and a courtyard cooled by a
central pool or fountain.
(Author's photograph)

It is unclear how much damage was done to local life by enemy raids, though many towns all along the Mongol and Armenian frontier seem to have been virtually empty except for their Mamluk garrisons. Even Aleppo was slow to recover from the Mongol occupation of 1260–61 and several years passed before its walls, citadel and main mosque were repaired, despite the fact that they were the main symbols of Islamic government authority.

The Mamluks' Mediterranean coastal cities faced comparable threats from crusader and European pirate raids. Not surprisingly, several of their arsenals were filled with abundant military stores. The arsenal of Alexandria contained 60,000 arrows, many bows, other weapons, armour, siege and incendiary equipment, according to the early 14th-century Muslim chronicler Shihab al-Din Ahmad al-Nuwayri. Nevertheless, Mamluk Alexandria was only defended by a small force plus local volunteers, so perhaps such stores may have been intended for use by a relief army rather than the resident garrison. The Genoese naval raiding party that attacked a fortified tower at Sidon in 1383 only seems to have been resisted by a small force, which suffered heavily from the crossbowmen – the most important offensive element in the Genoese fleet (Ashtor and Kedar 1975, pp. 19–21).

The penultimate Mamluk ruler, Sultan Qansawh II al-Ghawri (1501–16), probably intended his rebuilt fort of Burj al-Tina on the northern coast of Sinai to serve as both a command post and a defensive position. At first its distinctive outer octagonal wall was probably the main line of defence, perhaps with a few light cannon. Little more than a decade later, when an Ottoman force approached, the focus of defence may have shifted to the inner octagon, where additional cannon may now have been sited on the roof (Tamari 1978, pp. 13–23).

The heyday of the *ahdath* urban militia had passed by the time the Mamluk sultanate replaced the Ayyubids, first in Egypt and then in Syria. Nevertheless, urban militias and religiously motivated Muslim volunteers continued to have a role in siege warfare, both offensive and defensive, especially in Syria where there was frequent mention of *rijal al-thughur*, 'foot soldiers of the frontiers', during frontier wars against the Mongol Il-Khanate. Under Qala'un, for example, infantry troops were taken from the fortified frontier towns to participate in military expeditions far from their home territory, including raids deep into enemy territory on the other side of the Euphrates.

A comparable militia reappeared in and around the city of Damascus somewhat later, though their effectiveness against full-scale enemy assaults was limited. Furthermore, these militias, which largely consisted of infantry archers, never formed part of the Mamluk sultanate's regular army and did not normally take part in military reviews. Militias had less of a role in Mamluk Egypt, yet they did play a part in the defence of exposed ports like Alexandria. In fact, the crusader naval assault upon that city in 1365 shows both the importance and the limitations of indigenous local forces. When the Christian vessels remained at sea and did not approach the harbour, the population and garrison of Alexandria feared that this was the prelude to an attack. The enemy ships entered the western harbour, used by foreign merchants, and attacked the fortified walls, but were driven off by archers. Believing they had won a victory, the local populace and defenders came out of the walls onto the peninsula to 'insult the Franks', as the Arab chroniclers put it. However, the crusaders returned, got ashore, and trapped many of the defenders on the peninsula. Meanwhile, other enemy ships sailed into the eastern harbour where the walls appear to have been undefended. The crusaders were therefore able to force an entry through the *Bab al-Diwan* or 'Customs Gate', from where they attacked the defenders from behind (Van Steenbergen 2003, pp. 125–29 and 134–35).

Despite this mixed record, the Mamluk ruling class started to change its policy, if not its prejudices, towards locally recruited militias in the later 15th century. This was most obvious where infantry from the highlands of Syria, Lebanon and Palestine were concerned. One reason was the increasing difficulty of purchasing real 'slave-recruits' from what is now southern Russia, the Ukraine and Caucasus, but the changing nature of siege warfare and the increasing use of firearms would also have contributed to changing attitudes.

The Mongols and after

After the collapse of the Il-Khan Mongol successor state, struggles for the domination of fortified cities tended to be settled outside their walls – sometimes far away. The fate of Harat, for example, often depended upon the outcome of battles fought near two strategic bridges three and five kilometres from the city. Those seeking to take or dominate Harat generally relied upon imposing a blockade, devastating the surrounding agricultural zone while simultaneously conducting negotiations with whoever currently held the fortifications.

Harat was one of the strongest cities of the Kart dynasty (1245–1389) which ruled much of eastern Iran and northern Afghanistan. Even Timur-i Lang, with his huge army and bloodcurdling reputation, was unable to take Kart cities before 1381, when his reputation finally induced the population of Harat to open their gates. Terror was, in fact, one of the strongest weapons in Timur's armoury, especially when attacking fortified places. On several occasions the local population refused to take part in the defence of their own town for fear of what Timur-i Lang would do if he won. When Timur invaded Syria the local people were again sometimes too afraid to support the Mamluk garrisons who wanted to defend them.

In 1393, Timur-i Lang, having failed to take the mountain-top castle of al-Naja in Luristan and being unable to maintain his army in the field any longer, ordered the construction of a counter-castle so that the siege could continue. In fact 12 years passed before al-Naja capitulated. Such counter-castles, like other distant or isolated fortified positions, could only be held if

Mongol siege of the 'Assassin' cave fortress of Maymun Diz in 1256

Little remains of the once imposing citadel overlooking Mosul, though some of the city's fortifications beside the River Tigris can still be seen in the foreground. (Author's photograph)

Until the advent of longer-range cannon, the garrison of this 14th-century tower and surrounding walls could not realistically have closed the entrance to the harbour of Kududasi. (Author's photograph)

Timur's troops controlled the surrounding countryside and the territory between such positions and the main centres of Timurid power. The 'Fort of Issuk Kul' (Ysyk-Köl), built for Timur on the north side of the mountain lake of the same name in Kyrgyzstan, was particularly reliant upon supplies of food and munitions brought by friendly forces. Further west, overlooking the Syr Darya River, the strongly fortified town of Shahrukhia is said to have served as the muster point for the 'right wing' of Timurid army. In strategic terms this envisaged Timur's forces facing north or east, and consequently Shahrukhia was an assembly point for Timur's unfulfilled campaign towards China.

F   MONGOL SIEGE OF THE 'ASSASSIN' CAVE FORTRESS OF MAYMUN DIZ IN 1256

Cave fortresses, known as *shaqif* in Arabic, were common in many parts of the Middle East, but none seem to have been as elaborate as Maymun Diz in northern Iran. Its remains show that, in addition to extending, deepening and elaborating the natural caves, much was added to the front of the cliff using friable conglomerate rock from the site. This reconstruction is based upon Andrew Garai's in Willey 2005 (p. 117), with minor alterations. The castle was entered via a narrow path along the cliff face (centre right), before passing through an arch. In addition to passages, rooms and water-storage cisterns, there were several corridors wholly or partially inside the cliff face. These 'man-made' structures were originally covered with plaster and, until the development of larger counterweight stone-throwing siege weapons, Maymun Diz was virtually impregnable. The Mongol commander Hülegü and his Chinese siege engineers probably established their positions on relatively level ground from where Maymun Diz was in range of their new weapons. Inside the caves, fires are burning, caused by javelin-sized incendiary arrows shot by the Mongols' *kaman-i gav* giant crossbows.

Almost half a century later, Ahmad of Farghana found himself facing Timur's grandson and successor, the scholar-prince Ulugh Beg (1447–79). Being in the weaker position, Ahmad left garrisons in several forts then retreated into the mountains – a strategy that had been used since almost the beginning of recorded history in Central Asia. A few years later another Timurid civil war saw Husayn Bayqara besieging the fortified city of Harat, then held for the Timurid sultan Abu Sa'id. Each gate was commanded by an *amir*, the defenders reportedly working day and night to erect outworks and bastions. A reserve force was kept on alert within the city to help any threatened gate or wall. Husayn Bayqara had hoped for a peaceful surrender so did not attack at once, while the defenders stationed 'spies' outside the city. They reported that Husayn Bayqara intended to ride with a relatively small bodyguard to bathe, perhaps in a nearby stream or pool. So the defenders set up an ambush consisting of heavily armoured, spear-armed cavalry. However, this was driven off and they retreated, followed by some of Husayn Bayqara's men until the latter were forced back by archers on the walls of Harat. Seizing the opportunity, Husayn Bayqara sent troops to assault the Firuzabad Gate, which was defended by a unit commanded by an *amir* named Ahmad Hajji. The attackers successfully broke in and Harat fell.

Another siege from this period sheds further light on the conduct of such operations during the Timurid period. In 1463–64 Husayn Bayqara was still trying to win control of the Timurid state in Central Asia. This time he attacked Khiva, whose citadel was held by rebels under Nur Sa'id Shadman. Attempting to use guile rather than brute force, Husayn Bayqara sent a few troops, who rode donkeys and had their armour hidden beneath old clothes. They got into the citadel and seized control of an entrance, whereupon 27 more heavily armoured but similarly disguised troops emerged from a nearby hiding place to attack the citadel. At the same time, the rest of Husayn Bayqara's army hurried forward from a greater distance. The result was a fierce fight inside the city against the local infantry of Khiva, who eventually managed to force the attackers to retreat.

Accounts of siege warfare in the later medieval Islamic states of India show it to have been similar to that in the Timurid state, but with one particularly distinctive local feature – namely the use of elephants as live battering rams against fortified gates. This in turn accounted for the presence of remarkably massive spiked defences on such gates, and elephant armour, which often included very strong head protection.

AFTERMATH

As elsewhere in the world, the medieval fortifications of the Middle East continued to be used if they remained useful, or were abandoned, neglected or demolished if they were not. The fate of urban fortifications also reflected the changing importance of a town or city. In the eastern Arabian region of Oman, for example, the once flourishing coastal city of Qalhat eventually fell as a result of increasing hostility between its mercantile population and the tribal interior, while there is evidence of a major earthquake in the late 15th century. Qalhat was then sacked by the Portuguese in 1508, after which its commercial importance was eclipsed by that of nearby Muscat, now capital of the Sultanate of Oman.

In Egypt the citadel of Cairo remained a major fortress and military centre until modern times. Consequently most of Sultan al-'Adil's buildings within the fortifications were replaced by newer structures during the Mamluk sultanate; several Mamluk buildings were then replaced by those of the Ottoman Turks, most of which were in turn replaced during Muhammad 'Ali's massive reconstruction programme during the 19th century. Even today modern additions to the citadel, such as a theatre, are useful for the people of Cairo but have damaged certain historical remains. In contrast, in Alexandria changes in military technology resulted in very little remaining of the medieval urban fortifications, though the late Mamluk fortress of Qayit Bay was

The 14th-century castle of Ramana near Baku has been extensively restored. Though built of stone, its continuous machicolations are similar to comparable mud-brick machicolations in Yazd. (Angus Hay)

barely used by the Ottoman Turks after they took over Egypt in 1517 and was left largely unchanged. Not far away, the Qayit Bay fort just north of Rashid (Rosetta) was considerably strengthened after Napoleon occupied Egypt, though subsequent erosion by the River Nile has once again exposed part of the original structure, whilst also demolishing other sections.

In greater Syria the outer walls of the monumental urban citadels of Aleppo and Damascus remain largely intact, and although their interior structures were massively changed during the Ottoman period some buildings survive. Nothing of the present barbican of the citadel of Damascus seems to date from the Ayyubid period, though the structure which replaced it appears to be very similar. The very damaged north gate is also interesting because the Ayyubid version still exists inside the Mamluk one, while substantial fragments of the earlier Seljuk north gate have also been identified. Most of the citadel's Ayyubid and Mamluk walls and towers also survive except on the west, which was severely damaged by an earthquake in 1759. Here a lost tower was recently rebuilt upon its old foundations, based upon its surviving neighbours.

The almost complete city walls, towers and gates of Damascus make the Syrian capital one of the most fascinating cities in the world. Nevertheless, these urban fortifications inevitably suffered from wars, earthquakes and the ravages of urban development until the entire Old City was declared a UNESCO World Heritage Site. Before then, the upper part of the Bab al-Salamah, which is regarded as the purest Ayyubid gate in Damascus, was heavily but reasonably accurately restored in 1948.

In Lebanon the crusader castle of Tripoli was considerably modified by the Mamluks then repaired by the Ottomans shortly after their conquest, as recorded in an inscription dating from 1521 above the main gate. Thereafter, Tripoli remained a key element in the Ottoman empire's coastal defence system. There was similar extensive rebuilding of the late Mamluk fort at Aqaba in southern Jordan following the Ottoman conquest. This was a process that continued into the 19th century with further modifications to the Mamluk walls and turrets; the north-eastern and south-eastern towers were resurfaced, changing their shapes from polygonal to rounded, along with other changes to the gate and interior *iwan* or arched recess.

In northern Iraq the citadel of Mosul had been destroyed by the Mongols and thereafter was hardly used until 1625 when the Ottoman Turks restored a small part of what had been an extensive fortification. This was seriously damaged yet again during World War I. Not far away the superbly carved early 13th-century gate of the mountain-top town of 'Amadiyah collapsed

A fort built north of Rashid (Rosetta) during the very late Mamluk period was substantially altered during the Napoleonic occupation of Egypt. The original round southern tower has since been uncovered, whereas the western tower is still encased within a Napoleonic bastion. (Author's photograph)

some time during the 1960s, supposedly because of heavy snowfall but possibly as a result of the prolonged war between the Iraqi government and Kurdish separatists.

The once extensive fortified city of Kufa was largely abandoned by the end of the 12th century, though the Persian scholar al-Qazwini, describing the country for its new Mongol rulers in the 13th century, wrote that the important agricultural centre of Kufa still had ramparts 18,000 paces in circumference. A few generations later the great traveller Ibn Battuta indicated that Kufa was ruined, but not entirely dead. Nothing remained of the fortified Qasr al-'Imara governor's palace except its foundations, though the city's markets still thrived. Also in southern Iraq, the early Islamic city of Wasit was almost entirely abandoned after the River Tigris changed its course during the 16th and 17th centuries, literally leaving the city high and dry.

Many of the fortified cities of Iran and Afghanistan went into steep decline after the Mongol invasions, and then suffered again at the hands of Timur-i

G THE FORTRESS OF ALEXANDRIA HARBOUR, LATE 15TH CENTURY

The fortress of Qayit Bay, who ruled Egypt and Syria from 1468 to 1496, was built over the ruins of the ancient *pharos* or lighthouse of Alexandria. Qayit Bay wanted to protect the vital harbour and port at a time when the Mediterranean was dominated by European fleets, and this fortress was completed within two years. From the start, Qayit Bay's great fortress was designed to house cannon to counter the guns of European pirates and potentially crusader fleets. Most would have been placed in the outer walls and half-round towers. Meanwhile,

the tall central keep was traditional, perhaps being influenced by contemporary Italian and French citadels. Despite modern restoration, the late-15th-century fortress looked much as it does today. The original gate-complex survives, though the approach bridge and moat have changed. Old illustrations also permit a reconstruction of the great minaret and the smaller 'lighthouse tower' with its brazier and flag on top. The eastern harbour was reserved for Islamic shipping but its foreshore has now been replaced by a modern quay.

G

Lang. Isfahan only really revived under the Safavids, who ruled Iran from the 16th to early 18th centuries, when it became home to some of the world's most beautiful and delicate Islamic architecture. Yazd's remarkable and largely mud-brick fortifications remained in good repair well into the 19th century. With a circumference of 4km, they and the doubled wall of the inner city are amongst the most dramatic sights in Iran, while the walls of Yazd's citadel still rise almost 15m in height. The fortifications of Bam, in the far south-east of Iran, were the most picturesque of all until they were virtually obliterated in the 2003 earthquake. Defending a major strategic and commercial centre, Bam's citadel had been famous since the 10th century. It served as a major bastion against invaders from the east and also enclosed one of the city's three main mosques along with various bazaars. But because of its continuing strategic importance, Bam's fortifications were updated well into the 19th century, and the defences that were lost in the recent earthquake were mostly 16th-century Safavid.

The process of refortification and updating was similar in Islamic Central Asia. Here the devastation caused by the Mongols became proverbial, whereas Timur-i Lang, though an equally ruthless conqueror, developed some of its cities as remarkable centres of architecture and culture. After the Mongols sacked Samarqand, for example, a new city eventually developed on the western side of the now abandoned old city, in what had been one of the earlier suburbs. Meanwhile, most of the largely mud-brick urban defences that can still be seen around parts of Bukhara are again not medieval. They largely date from the 18th-century (partially built upon earlier) massive, pisé, puddled clay ramparts. The new but very traditional *Ark* of Bukhara is similarly on the site of an older citadel, this also being the case with the defences and *Ark* or citadel of Khiva.

In addition to devastation at the hands of man, the old city of Urgench suffered an inexorable decline because the neighbouring river shifted its course. As a result, Kunya (Old) Urgench was replaced by Khiva as the capital of Khwarazm during the 16th and 17th centuries. Further east the fortified town and military base of Shahrukhia, named after Timur-i Lang's first son, continued to be an important location under the Shibanids (Uzbek

The medieval fortifications of the port-city of Rashid (Rosetta) illustrated by H. Boot in the 19th century, showing a gate and flanking towers that have since disappeared.

Turks) during the 16th century. It then declined during the wars that ravaged Central Asia in the 17th century; so much so that its name was almost forgotten, the deserted site becoming known as Sharkia. River erosion early in the 20th century revealed the site once again, enabling archaeologists to identify it as the lost city of Shahrukhia.

BIBLIOGRAPHY

Adams, W.Y., *Qasr Ibrim: the Late Medieval Period* (Egyptian Exploration Society, London 1996).

Agius, D., 'Medieval Qalhat', in H.P. Ray (ed.), *Archaeology of Seafaring in the Indian Ocean* (Delhi 1999), pp. 173–220.

Alfy, A.M.S. el- and S. el-Alfy, *Island of Pharaoun, Citadel of Salahal-Din* (Cairo 1986).

Allen, T., *Ayyubid Architecture* (web publication, Occidental, California 1996).

Allen, T., *Timurid Herat* (Wiesbaden 1983).

Ashtor, E. and B.Z. Kedar, 'Una Guerra fra Genova e i Mamlucchi negli anni 1380', *Archivio Storico Italiano*, p. 133 (1975).

Barthoux, J., 'Description d'une forteresse de Saladin decouverte au Sinai', *Syria*, 3 (1922), pp. 44–57.

Braune, M., 'Die Stadtmauer von Damaskus', *Damaszener Mitteilungen*, 11 (1999), pp. 67–88.

Braune, M., *Untersuchungen zur mittelalterliche Befestigung in Nordwest-Syrien: Die Assassinenberg Masyaf* (Damascus 1985).

Brun, P., 'From Arrows to Bullets: the fortifications of Abdullah Khan Kala (Merv, Turkmenistan)', *Antiquity*, 79 (2005), pp. 616–24.

Brun, P., 'The Medieval Fortifications', in G. Herrmann et al (eds.), 'The International Merv Project: Preliminary Report on the Ninth Year (2000)', *Iran*, 39 (2001), pp. 25–34.

Burton-Page, J., 'A Study of Fortification in the Indian Subcontinent from the Thirteenth to the Eighteenth Century AD', *Bulletin of the School of Oriental and African Studies*, 23 (1960), pp. 508–22.

Buryakov, Y.F. et al, *The Cities and Routes of the Great Silk Road* (Tashkent 1999).

Clavijo (C.R. Markham tr.), *Narrative of the Embassy of Ruy Gonzales de Clavijo to the Court of Timour at Samarqand A.D. 1403–6* (London 1859).

Combe, E., 'Le Fort de Qayt Bay à Rosetta', and A. De Cosson, 'Notes on the Forts of Alexandria and Environs: Fort Qaitbai, Rosetta', *Bulletin de la Société Royale d'Archéologie d'Alexandrie*, n.s. 10 (1938–39), pp. 312–24.

Creswell, K.A.C., 'Fortification in Islam before AD 1200', *Proceedings of the British Academy*, 38 (1952), pp. 89–125.

Creswell, K.A.C., *The Muslim Architecture of Egypt* (reprint, New York 1978).

Duggan, T.M.P., 'The Plaster and Paintwork on 13th century Rum Seljuk hans', *Adalya* (forthcoming).

Edwards, R.W., 'Medieval Architecture in the Oltu-Penek Valley. A Preliminary Report on the Marchlands of Northeast Turkey', *Dumbarton Oaks Papers*, 39 (1985).

Ellenblum, R., 'Who built Qal'at al Subayba?' *Dumbarton Oaks Papers*, 43 (1989) pp. 103–12.

Erdmann, K., *Das anatolische Karavansaray des 13. Jahrhunderts* (Berlin 1961).

Faucherre, N., J. Mesqui and N. Prouteau (eds.), *La Fortification au Temps des Croisades* (Rennes 2004): particularly, J. Bylinski, 'Three Minor Fortresses in the Realm of Ayyubid rulers of Homs in Syria ', pp. 151–64; P. Dangles, 'La refortification d'Afamiyya', pp. 189–204; H. Hanisch, 'The Works of al-Malik al-'Adil in the Citadel of Harran', pp. 165–78; A. Hartmann-Virnisch, 'Les portes ayyoudides de la citadelle de Damas', pp. 287–311; C. Tonghini and M. Montevecchi, 'The castle of Shayzar', pp. 137–50; V. Vachon, 'Les châteaux Ismâ'iliens du Djabal Bahrâ', pp. 219–41; C. Yovitchich, 'La citadelle de Bosra', pp. 205–17.

Ferté, H., *Vie de Sultan Hossein Baikara* (Paris 1896).

Gardin, J.C., *Lashkari Bazar: Une residence royale ghaznevide* (Paris 1963).

Hanisch, H., *Die ayyubidischen Torelagen der Zitadelle von Damaskus* (Wiesbaden 1996).

Hanisch, H., 'Die seldschukischen Anlagen der Zitadelle von Damaskus', *Damaszener Mitteilungen*, 6 (1992), pp. 479–99.

Harrison, P., *Castles of God: Fortified Religious Buildings of the World* (Woodbridge 2004).

Hartal, M., *The al-Subayba (Nimrod) Fortress (IAA Reports, 11)* (Jerusalem 2001).

Herrmann, G. (et al.), 'The International Merv Project: Preliminary Report on the Ninth Year (2000)', *Iran*, 39 (2001).

Homés-Fredericq, D., and J.B. Hennessy (eds.), *Archaeology of Jordan (Akkadica, Supplementum) III* (Leuven 1986–89): particularly, R.M. Brown, 'Kerak Castle', II/i, pp. 341–47; 'Shawbak', II/ii, pp. 559–66.

H. Kennedy (ed.), *Muslim Military Architecture in Greater Syria* (Leiden 2006): particularly, S. Berthier, 'La Citadelle de Damas', pp. 151–64; S. Gelichi, 'The Citadel of Harim', pp. 184–200; J. Gonnella, 'The Citadel of Aleppo', pp. 165–75; S. Heidemann, 'The Citadel of al-Raqqa and the Fortifications in the Middle Euphrates Area', pp. 122–50; B. Major, 'Medieval Cave Fortifications on the Upper Orontes Valley', pp. 251–68; B. Michaudel, 'The Development of Islamic Military Architecture during the Ayyubid and Mamluk Reconquests of Frankish Syria', pp. 106–21; N. O. Rabbat, 'The Militarization of Taste in Medieval Bilad al-Sham', pp. 84–105; Y. Tabbaa, 'Defending Ayyubid Aleppo', pp. 176–83; C. Tonghini and M. Montevecchi, 'The Castle of Shayzar: the fortifications of the access system', pp. 201–24; C. Yovitchich, 'The Tower of Aybak in 'Ajlun Castle', pp. 225–42.

Kritzeck, J. and R. Bayly Winder (eds.), *The World of Islam: Studies in Honour of Philip H. Hitti* (London 1959).

Mackenzie, N.D., 'The Fortifications of al-Qahira (Cairo) under the Ayyubids', in H. Dajani-Shakeel and R.A. Messier (eds.), *Jihad and its Times* (Ann Arbor 1991), pp. 71–95.

Maulana Minhaj al-Din (H.G. Raverty tr.), *Tabakat-i Nasiri: A General History of the Muhammadan Dynasties of Asia* (reprint New Delhi 1970).

Mesqui, J., 'Le Château de Saône/Sahyon', *Histoire et Images Médiévales Thématiques*, 11 (Nov. 2007–Jan. 2008), pp. 46–55.

Michaudel, B., 'The Development of Islamic Military Architecture during the Ayyubid and Mamluk Reconquests of Frankish Syria', in H. Kennedy (ed.), *Muslim Military Architecture in Greater Syria* (Leiden 2006).

Mouton, J-M. (et al.), 'Le route de Saladin (tariq Sadr wa Ayla) au Sinai', *Annales Islamologiques*, 30 (1996), pp. 41–70.

Padines, S. (et al), 'La muraille ayyoubide du Cairo...', *Annales Islamologiques*, 36 (2002), pp. 292.

Piana, M. (ed.), *Burgen und Städte der Kreuzzugzeit* (Petersberg 2008).

Pope, A.U., 'Fortifications', in A.U. Pope (ed.), *A Survey of Persian Art* (London 1939), pp. 1,241–45.

Rabbat, N.O., 'The Militarization of Taste in Medieval Bilad al-Sham', in H. Kennedy (ed.), *Muslim Military Architecture in Greater Syria* (Leiden 2006)

Sadek, Hassan Effendi, 'Salah al-Din's Fort on Ras el Gindi in Sinai', *Bulletin de l'Institut d'Egypte*, 2 (1919–20), pp. 111–19.

Sauvaget, J., 'Notes sur les défenses de Marine de Tripoli', *Bulletin du Musée de Beyrouth*, 2 (1938), pp. 1–25.

Sauvaget, J., *La Poste aux chevaux dans L'Empire des Mamelouks* (Paris 1941).

Schlumberger, D., 'Palais Ghaznévide de Lashkari Bazar', *Syria*, 29 (1952).

Schlumberger, D., *Lashkari Bazar* (Paris 1978).

Tamari, S., 'Qal'at al Tina in Sinai…', *Annali, Istituto Orientale di Napoli*, 38 (1978), pp. 1–78.

Usamah Ibn Munqidh (P.H. Hitti tr.), *Memoires of an Arab-Syrian Gentleman* (Princeton 1929).

Van Ess, M., *Heliopolis-Baalbek, 1898-1998, Rediscovering the Ruins* (Berlin 1998).

Van Steenbergen, J., 'The Alexandrian Crusade (1365) and the Mamluk Sources: Reassessment of the Kitab al-Ilman of an-Nuwayri al-Iskandarani', in K. Ciggar et al (eds.), *East and West in the Crusades; Context, Contacts, Confrontations, vol. 3* (Leuven 2003).

Voisin, J-C., 'Pour une nouvelle lectures des fortifications médiévales au sud-Liban', *Annales d'Histoire et d'Archéologie (Université Saint-Joseph)*, 8–9 (1997–98), pp. 49–73.

Whitehouse, D.B., 'Excavations at Siraf: Sixth Interim Report', *Iran*, 12 (1974), pp. 1–30.

Willey, P., *Eagle's Nest: Ismaili Castles in Iran and Syria* (New York 2005).

William of Rubruck (P. Jackson tr.), *The Mission of Friar William of Rubruck: his journey to the court of the Great Khan Möngke 1253–1255* (London 1990).

Ziadeh, N.A., *Urban Life in Syria under the Early Mamluks* (Westport 1953).

INDEX

References to illustrations are shown in **bold**.
Plates are shown with page and caption locators
in brackets.

Abu'l-Hassan 'Ali al-Harawi 49
Agzikarakhan **15**, 35
Ajlun castle, Jordan 24
Alamut, 'Assassin' castle 16, **32**
Alanya 12
Alara Khan 27
Aleppo 12, 17–18, 22, 24–5, 33, 36, 41, 51, 52
    citadel **5**, **47**, 57
Alexandria 25, 36, **45**(44), 52, 53
    Qayit Bay 25, 57, **59**(58)
Altuntash, governor 20
'Amadiyah 57–8
Anatolia 21, 35, 49
Aqaba 57
Ardabil citadel 27
Armenia 7, 13, 16
'Assassin castles' 15–16, **54**(55)
Aswan, Egypt 12
Atabegs 17–21, 32–7
Ayyubids 22, 24–5, 37, 39, 49–53
Azaz 22

Baalbak **19**(18), 20, 47–8
Badr al-Jamari, wazir 7–8, 9, 12, 13
Baghdad 8, 12, 15, 17, 22, 49
Baku 17, 20
Balis 13
Baltit castle 50
Bam 60
al-Bara 41
Baybars, Sultan of Egypt 25, 50
Bijapur 29
Bilbays fortress 9
al-Bira 50
Bitlis fortress 39
building materials,
    brick 9, 13, 14, 22, 27, 28
    external plaster 22, **27**
    stone 9, 17, 22, 27
Bukhara 17, 60
Burj al-Tina 52
Busra 20, 26, 32, 39

Cairo 7, 25, 26, 30–1, 33, 57
    citadels **5**, 24, 37, **44**, 56–7
    walls and gates 9, **10–11**(9), 12, **12**, 13,
        30, 31
caravansarai 27, 35
citadels 5, 25, 31, **32**, 40
Clavijo, Ruy Gonzales de 28, 41
crusaders (Franks) 22, 24, 36, 44, 47, 53

Dalautabad 30
Damascus 9, 17, 18, 36, 40, 53
    canals 21, **30**
    citadels **5**, 9, 24, **26**, 33, 37, 57
Darband (Derbent) 20, **24**
Delhi 29, 41
Dimyat (Damietta), siege of 49–50
Diyar Bakir (Amida) 21, 48, 50

Egypt 5, 7–8, 9, 12

Fabri, Felix 25
Fatimid caliphate 7, 8, 13, 30
Fifth Crusade 49–50
First Crusade 8, 41–2

Firuzkuh, citadel 28
fortifications **12**, **13**, 26, 28, 56–60
    late medieval **45**(44)
    palaces 5, 17, 29, 33

gates 9, 12, 30
Ghazna 14, 17, 33
Gulbarga 29

al-Hadba citadel 41
Harat 14, **18**, **39**, 40, 49, 53
Harran citadel **5**, 24
Hassakih citadel 8
Hassan Ibn Mismar 12–13
Hisn Kayfa (Hasankayf) **35**
Husayn Bayqara 56

Ibn Battuta 58
Ibn Jubayr 17
Ibn Sasra, *Chronicle of Damascus* 40
Ibn Shihna 25
Ibn Tiqtaqa 49
Ibn Urunbugha al-Zardkash 50
India, Islamic 28–30, **38**, 41, 56
Inqirata, *khan* 13
Iran 15, **34**, 60
Isfahan 14, 17, 60
Isma'ili caliphate 15–17

Jajarm, Iran 16, 41
Jakam min'Iwad 25
Jalal al-Din castle 16, **32**, 41
Jam 17
Jarash 8, **32**
Jazirat Fara'un (Qal'at Ayla) **23**(22), 24, **51**
Jazirat Ibn Umar 17
Jerusalem 8, 25

Karaman castle **46**(47)
Kayseri 22, 37, 49
Khan al-Arus 35
khans 13, 16, 22, 35
Khiva 56, 60
Kish (Shakhrisabz) 16
Konya 37
Kududsai harbour 55
Kufa 58
Kulan 12

la Brocquière, Bertrandon de 40
Lal Kot 29
Lashkar-i Bazar **5**, 14

Mamluks **5**, 25–7, 39–41, 50–3
Manakhur 13
Manzikirt, battle of (1071) 8
al-Maqrizi 13, 31
Mardin 21
Marw-i Shahijan **12**, 13–15, **48**
    Abdullah Khan Qal'a 28, **45**(44)
Mas'ud III, Sultan 33
Masyaf castle **32**
Mayadin 39
maydans 35–6
Maymun Diz, 'Assassin' fortress **54**(55)
Middle East, maps 6, 7, **38**
minarets 16–17, **27**, **48**
Mongols 27–8, 39–41, 49–51, 58, 60
    warfare 53, 55–6
Mosul 8, 17, 27–8, 36, 41
    citadel 55, 57

Narin, Meybod castle **29**
Nishapur 32, 35
Nur al-Din 17–18, 20, 33, 35–6

Palmyra 17
Pir Sadat 16
postal services 27, 40, 50

Qa'in 15, **43**
Qal'at Jabar **21**, **40**
Qalhat, port-city **4**, 17, 56
Qasr al-Hayr al-Sharqi 14
Qasr al-Tina **45**(44)
Qazwin 14
al-Qazwini, Hamidullah Mustawfi 13, 20,
    27–8, 58

Rahba castle (Qal'at Rahba) 17, 22, 31, **32**, 39,
    40, 50
Ramana castle 57
Ramlah 48
Raqqa citadel 22
Rashid (Rosetta) 25, **45**(44), 57, 58, 60

Sadr castle (Qal'at al-Gindi) **14**, **26**
Sahyun (Saone) 24, **52**
Saladin **22**, 35, 37, 49, 51
Salkhad citadel 12–13, **52**
Samarqand **12**, 41, **43**, 60
Second Crusade 9, 36
Seljuks 8, 21–5, 32–7
    Great Seljuk caliphate 13–17, 33, 44,
        47–9
    Sultanate of Rum 21, 36–7, **47**, 49
Shahrukhia 28, **45**(44), 55, 60–1
Shayzar citadel **31**, 31, **32**, 32, 44, 47
Shumaymis castle **32**
siege warfare 49–50
    artillery 16, 26–7, 41, 43, 50
Sivas 37
Subayba castle 37, 39, **42**(43)
Sultan al-Nasir 25
Sultan Han *khan* 13
Sultaniya 28
Syria 8, 12–13, 31, 50, 53

Tashrabat *khan* 13
Timur-i Lang 16, 28, 41, 53, 55–6,
    58, 60
Tinnis fortress 9
Tirmidh (Termez) 14
towers 9, 12, 25–6
Tripoli 25, 26, **45**(44), 57
Turks 4–5, 35; *see also* Seljuks

Usama Ibn Munqidh 31, 44, 47

Vabkkent **27**

walls 9, 14–15, 25–6, 28, 29–30
warfare 41–56
Wasit 48, 58
water supplies 47–8
wazirs 7, 30
William of Rubruck, Friar 20

Yazd 13, 28, 37, 60
Ysyk-Köl (Issuk Kul) 55

Zangid dynasty 35, 36
Zivrik *khan* 13